CHARLES DICKENS

CHARLES DICKENS

BY

G. K. CHESTERTON

INTRODUCTION
by Steven Marcus

SCHOCKEN BOOKS · NEW YORK

First published 1906

First SCHOCKEN PAPERBACK edition 1965

Copyright © 1965 by Schocken Books Inc.
Library of Congress Catalog Card No. 65-14824
Manufactured in the United States of America

CONTENTS

INTRODUCTION

G. K. CHESTERTON'S work on Dickens is of considerable historical interest and importance. It was first published in 1906, a time when Dickens's reputation had dropped very low. This statement in itself requires some explanation. It does not mean that Dickens had ceased to be a popular favorite or that readers from all classes and divisions of life had stopped buying, borrowing, and reading his novels. They never have, and from the time Dickens began writing until today he remains the one *great* English novelist who is also an immense popular success. Nor does the statement mean that Dickens's reputation had declined everywhere; in fact throughout the latter part of the nineteenth century his stature as a writer had steadily grown in France, Germany, and Russia, so that at the time Chesterton set about his work Dickens had already come to be regarded on the Continent in the way that he is still regarded today — as that figure in English literature who, in virtue of creative and imaginative power, stands second only to Shakespeare. The statement does mean that Dickens had fallen into disrepute within a particular group in the English-speaking world.

This group may be defined as the educated or literary class of society; it largely consists of those persons who are engaged in the creation of literature — novelists, poets, dramatists — and of those who are otherwise in their professional lives connected with literary activity — critics, reviewers, teachers and professors, editors and publishers. This group is in modern society comparatively small in numbers, but its power of influence beyond its own sphere is disproportionately large. It is responsible for creating the literary or cultural consciousness of its time, for distinguishing what is good from what is bad, for maintaining certain traditions and their attendant values, and for sponsoring what is new and challenging. In the collective mind of this class in the English-speaking world at the turn of the century Dickens occupied a peripheral and even a contemptible place.

It is not difficult to explain or understand how this remarkable situation came about. In the first place, a creative figure of such magnitude and dominance as Dickens is bound in the course of time to provoke a dialectical response against and away from him. The dominance is experienced as domination, as stifling to further or new creative efforts. Henry James, who as a child first heard Dickens being read in the circle of his family, speaks of the obligation, the tyranny, under which Dickens had laid an entire epoch of readers. "He did too much for us . . .," James writes in his autobiography, "ever to leave us free — free of judgment, free of reaction, even should we care to be"; and he goes on to say that Dickens had entered unalterably "into the blood and bone of our intelligence," meaning the intelligence of his generation, and that Dickens was "the great actuality of the current imagination," meaning the literary and creative imagination of the whole middle of the nineteenth century. Such extraordinary power requires an equally extraordinary rejection, and as a young writer James wrote a review of *Our Mutual Friend* which was irreverent, destructive, excessive, and sometimes downright foolish. Its real point, however, was to get Dickens out of the way, to clear the decks, and to allow Henry James to become Henry James.

Literature when it is regarded historically usually proceeds by opposition. Opposition, however, is not supercession, and in

terms of the relative value or excellence of works of art there is
no such thing as progress. To think that a particular form of art
— in this instance the novel — which develops in time also improves or progresses, in any other sense than that of developing
new technical means for solving certain problems, is to reason
by false analogy. The novelists who came after Dickens had
their own separate interests and their own talents to exploit. In
such writers as George Eliot, Meredith, Hardy a.id Henry
James new areas of experience were brought within the range
of the novel and new techniques were invented for representing
them. In addition, during the late Victorian period certain
quasi-ideological movements in art began to form, and groups
of writers who represented the points of view of realism, and
naturalism, and aestheticism stepped forward with their own
claims. These claims had naturally to do with the priority and
superiority of the kind of art, the kind of novel, that each of
these movements represented. And as it always tends to happen
in matters of art, and as it happened in the case of the admirers
of the important novelists who followed Dickens, the value one
wishes to ascribe to one's own works or preferences seems to be
enhanced if one can simultaneously and radically devalue other
works and preferences both present and past. Dickens was the
most valued, admired, and influential English novelist of the
middle years of the nineteenth century; by the same token he
was the chief object of devaluation in that century's latter
decades. Finally, at about this time translations into English
began to be made of the great French and Russian novelists.
These too were acclaimed, and part of the use to which the ac-
claim was put was to make unfavorable comparisons between
these novelists — most of whom were fervent admirers of
Dickens — and Dickens. All of these matters working together
— along with others too complex to go into here — brought about
the circumstances in which Chesterton wrote his book.[1]

It should not be thought, however, that Chesterton was al-

---

[1]. The reader who is further interested in this side of the question should
consult George H. Ford's very useful *Dickens and his Readers; Aspects of
Novel-Criticism Since 1836* (Princeton, 1955).

together a voice crying in the wilderness. He is one of three important writers to insist on the greatness of Dickens at this time when most others were insisting on the opposite. The other two are George Gissing and George Bernard Shaw; the comments of both of these critics on Dickens still contain valuable material. Chesterton's book is distinguished by the size of the claim he makes for Dickens, by the vigor and idiosyncrasy with which that claim is advanced, and by the character and quality of the estimate of Dickens which he proposes. It is one of the first important modern estimates — or re-estimates — of Dickens, and it remains important in itself and in the challenge it offers to the reader today.

But the reader today will not merely feel challenged by this book. Unless I am mistaken he will find much to disagree with in it and a good deal that is annoying. It might be the better course to get these objections first out of the way. No one who reads this book today will fail to be both impressed and irritated by the way it is written, by its style. Chesterton thought and wrote in paradoxes, and his writing is characterized by the limitations which the addiction to any single mode of thought must entail. Edmund Wilson, in his own historic essay on Dickens, praises Chesterton but complains about his style, which he describes as "melting away into that pseudo-poetic booziness which verbalizes with large conceptions and ignores the most obtrusive actualities." Every page of this book is adorned, and every other page is merely littered, with these paradoxes. Some of them are brilliant — as in the passage dealing with Toots from *Dombey and Son*. Some of them merely get on one's nerves — as in the following two sentences from the first chapter. "One of the actual and certain consequences of the idea that all men are equal is immediately to produce very great men. . . . The best men of the Revolution were simply common men at their best." Both of these statements contain a portion of truth, but the form in which both are cast distorts the truth out of all proportion. The first is an enormous inflation, the hypostatization of an interesting speculation into something which resembles a cosmic law. The second does the reverse, and one feels that the paradox is here diminishing and shrinking the significance of the event it comments upon. The cumulative effect of such a procedure is to steadily increase the reader's resistance to it, until one greets each successive reversal or manipulation with a silent grunt which signifies, "No!" or "So what!" or "Who cares?" And this would be the lasting effect were Chesterton not regularly capable of overcoming himself, and by the sheer clarity of his insight, the freshness and sincerity of his interest in Dickens, and the vividness and gaiety with which he confronts both the reader and the material overcoming both as well.

The contemporary reader will also in all likelihood feel troubled at the way in which Chesterton's argument is constructed — rather, by the way it fails to fulfill current conventional expectations about construction. Chesterton is writing in an older form of literary composition or criticism. He ruminates, he associates, he lets his pen carry him where it will. He is often inconsequent, and his arguments are not conducted along large, distinct logical lines. He almost never enters upon the critical analysis of a specific text, and his conclusions do not arise immanently out of his handling of the concrete material, out of his demonstrations. These objections, which are made in behalf of the admirable austerity of modern literary criticism, certainly have their point. They may in part be met, however, if we consider that the logical procedures of modern criticism — which in any event had not yet been really developed — were not germane to Chesterton's purpose. His book is largely polemical and hortatory; it is a piece of literary propaganda on the highest level. And the reader will soon see that this work is not about Dickens alone. At certain points Dickens is only a pretext, a point of departure for Chesterton's presentation of his own views about this, that, and everything, about modern life in general. These views, it may be added, rarely fail to be of intrinsic interest.

When it comes to Dickens himself, Chesterton commits himself to certain notions which later criticism of Dickens has been unable to accept. The Dickens which Chesterton adores — it is not too strong a word — is the early Dickens, the Dickens of *Pickwick Papers, Nicholas Nickleby* and the other novels of the first half of Dickens's career. He does not really respond to the later works, although he admits their superiority in a "merely" technical sense. Dickens, he writes, "improves as an artist if not always as a creator." Modern comment has seen it necessary to dispute this opinion. It regards the novels of the second half of Dickens's career as distinctly superior to the early work. In addition, it has come to understand Dickens's career as an artist as — after that of Shakespeare's — one of the supreme instances of growth and development, of moral as well as creative development, in our language. I should say that I am in substantial agreement with these judgments, although Chesterton's book, it seems to me, remains genuinely useful as a reminder of the greatness, the uniqueness, the immense achievement of Dickens's earlier novels. Chesterton also accepted the old and cliché notion that Dickens was unable to construct a plot or manage a coherent narrative. He did not only accept it; he carried the idea to an extreme. "Dickens's work is not to be reckoned in novels at all," he writes. "Dickens's work is to be reckoned always by characters, sometimes by groups, oftener by episodes, but never by novels. . . . his novels are simply lengths cut from the flowing and mixed substance called Dickens." Although he is here trying to turn what is supposed to be a critical statement against Dickens into its opposite, the highest praise, and is speaking of Dickens as if he were great creating Nature itself — as the 18th century spoke of Homer and the 19th spoke of Shakespeare — modern criticism has found this kind of statement to be unacceptable as well. It has discovered that, far from being incoherent, Dickens's novels, including his early novels, are organized in the most remarkable and complex ways. Those plots that everyone used to complain about are now understood as poetic and symbolic in their functions; each novel is now seen to be underlaid by a whole series of interlocking and mutually reflecting themes which are expressed in the relations of the characters and their movement through the narrative. And Dickens's imagination as a novelist is now properly thought of as synthesizing the elements of his works with the kind of coherence, intensity, and density of meaning that we meet with only in the highest order of poetic and dramatic genius.

The discriminating reader will note these differences and defects, but will not be put off by them. He will understand them as incidental to the major thesis and the major contribution that this book has to offer.

Chesterton's central idea is that Dickens was an immense event, a cataclysm, an eruption, an era in English history. It is the largeness of scale, the immensity that attached to Dickens's career, that he reminds us of — in both the public life of culture and in literary history. Dickens, he characteristically writes, "led a mob. He did what no English statesman, perhaps, has really done; he called out the people. He was popular in a sense of which we moderns have not even a notion." This public success, he goes on to remark, "was a marvel and almost a monstrosity," and he notes what seems in some sense to have almost been true; that "in the days when Dickens's work was coming out in serial, people talked as if real life were itself the interlude between one issue of 'Pickwick' and another." Such statements serve to reveal the mythical quality of Dickens's life and career; Chesterton's remarks are half-mythological themselves, but in this instance the form in which they are put coincides with the whole tendency of Dickens's work and its reception. Chesterton also identifies Dickens as "deeply and radically English; the most English of our great writers," and he speaks at length of Dickens's special relation to the great masses of ordinary Englishmen. "He did not pity the people, or even champion the people, or even merely love the people . . . he was the people. He alone in our literature is the voice not merely of the social substratum, but even of the subconsciousness of the substratum." These assertions are advanced with typical exaggeration, and during the Marxist 30's a good deal of effort was

expended to demonstrate that Dickens did not really identify with
or write about "the people" — that is, the proletariat — and that
his attitudes were not theirs. The truth contained in such criticism was noted and assimilated, and as it was assimilated the
truth that is held in Chesterton's statements has in turn re-
emerged. This truth is exemplified in the wonderful passage of
hyperbole in which Chesterton describes the effect of Dickens's
death.

> He died in 1870; and the whole nation mourned for him as no public
> man has ever been mourned; for prime ministers and princes were
> private persons compared with Dickens. He had been a great popular
> king, like a king of some more primal age whom his people could come
> and see, giving judgment under an oak tree. . . . His obvious omni-
> presence in every part of public life was like the omnipresence of
> the sovereign. His secret omnipresence in every house and hut of
> private life was more like the omnipresence of a deity.

What Chesterton is trying to indicate is the depth to which
Dickens had penetrated into the general consciousness of England and Englishmen. His statements may also remind us of
how unthinkable the occurrence of such a writer is today.

The concrete side of this abstract or universal notion is that,
for Chesterton, Dickens embodied the spirit of the French Revolution in England. In Chesterton's view Dickens was "the living
expression" of native English radicalism as it took shape in the
decades following the upheavals in France and the Continent.
"He was the voice in England of this humane intoxication and
expansion. . . . His best books are a carnival of liberty, and there
is more of the real spirit of the French Revolution in *Nicholas
Nickleby* than in *A Tale of Two Cities.*" Dickens in other words
represents the breaking-out in England of the two great oppos-
ing impulses which animated the Revolution: the simultaneous
passion for individual liberty and for social equality — and the
belief that both could be achieved. In short he represents the
spirit of democracy. Chesterton resorts to a variety of arguments in making these points; some of these are convincing,
some less so. In discussing Dickens's "early radical indictments" of social abuses he remarks that "in his denunciations of

the Fleet Prison there was a great deal of the capture of the Bastille." One feels that here Chesterton has hit the nail on the head. Or when he distinguishes between the kind of radicalism Dickens represented and other more modern kinds, he says: "The old Radical did not feel exactly that he was 'in revolt'; he felt if anything that a number of idiotic institutions had revolted against reason and against him." What Chesterton has caught here is the confidence, the optimism, the sense of possibility with which early social radicalism was imbued and which Dickens, in the first half of his career, may be said to have shared. Similarly, Chesterton suggests that the multiplicity and variety of the characters in Dickens's novels, the intense individuality of even the most minor of minor persons, has a large social meaning. "In this democratic aspect of the interest and variety of all men, there is, of course, no democrat so great as Dickens."

Another side of this insight is disclosed when we say that Chesterton was right in emphasizing so strongly Dickens's great feeling for common humanity. Dickens saw, he writes, "that there was a secret thing called humanity, to which both extreme socialism and extreme individualism were profoundly and inexpressibly indifferent, and that this permanent and presiding humanity was the thing he happend to understand." And when he states that "the intoxicating variety of men" constituted Dickens's "vision and conception of human brotherhood," he is saying a similar thing. But Dickens did not merely have such a vision; he was also able to create it for others, and in a special way. He was able to take characters like Toots, characters whom, when we meet them in life, we pity, we avoid, we despise, we are embarrassed and frightened by — characters who in their weakness, or openness, or foolishness, or degradation are too much for us and from whom we turn away — and make them live for us in a new way.

But Dickens does not despise him. Without denying one of the dreary details which make us avoid the man, Dickens makes him a man whom we long to meet. He does not gloss over one of his dismal deficiencies, but he makes them seem suddenly like violent virtues that we would go to the world's end to see. Without altering one fact, he manages to alter the whole atmosphere, the whole universe of Toots. He makes us not only like, but love, not only love, but reverence this little dunce and cad. The power to do this is a power truly and literally to be called divine.

For once Chesterton is not exaggerating, and this ability to gaze unwaveringly into human folly and misery and see its connection with ourselves is one of Dickens's greatest gifts to us. This feeling for common humanity is in English shared in its full depth only by Shakespeare and Dickens. And Chesterton is correct to connect it at several points not only to the French Revolution and the radical humanitarianism of Dickens's time, but to Dickens's Christianity, his literal, his primitive Christianity. Dostoevsky, who called Dickens his master, also called him "the great Christian." He knew whereof he spoke.

When it comes to specific literary comment and insight, Chesterton is equally interesting. As I have mentioned, *Pickwick Papers* is his special favorite, and his comments on it are among the best ever made. He understands that in some way this first work of genius transcends the genre in which it is supposed to belong and becomes "something nobler than a novel, for no novel with a plot and proper termination could emit that sense of ever lasting youth — a sense as of the gods gone wandering in England." And he also tries to explain how it is that he and other Englishmen have refused to believe that the characters in *Pickwick Papers* were contained by the novel and came to an end when it did. "But we know he did not stop there. We know he broke out, that he took again the road of high adventures; we know that if we take it ourselves in any acre of England, we may come suddenly upon him in a lane." This ability of Dickens's to create almost as Nature does is dwelled on constantly by Chesterton. In our own time we have concentrated on the opposite — on Dickens's genius as a deliberate artist — and so Chesterton's remarks are a refreshing reminder.

Chesterton also saw things in Dickens that no one had seen before, and he anticipated certain modern attitudes towards Dickens for which he should be credited with priority. He was the first one to say that "Dickens did not strictly make a literature; he made a mythology," and that "Dickens was a mythologist." It took the whole creation of modern literature, it took Eliot and Joyce and Kafka and Mann and Faulkner, to demonstrate just how profoundly mythological Dickens' talent was. Chesterton did not precisely mean what we mean when he speaks of mythology, but he is not too far from our meaning either. He states of *Pickwick Papers,* for example, that "the strange and stirring discovery which Dickens made was this — that having chosen a fat old man of the middle classes as a good thing of which to make a butt, he found that a fat old man of the middle classes is the very best thing of which to make a romantic adventurer. *Pickwick* is supremely original in that it is the adventures of an old man." And he goes on to say that Mr. Pickwick is the type of a "true and neglected thing, the romance of the middle classes." Eighty-five years later, James Joyce was to create another romantic adventurer and another romance of the middle classes in an equally unlikely person, a middle-aged Dublin Jew named Leopold Bloom. And like Dickens before him Joyce was able to create Bloom only through his symbiotic relation to a younger man: Mr. Pickwick cannot live without Sam Weller; Bloom is completed by Stephen Dedalus.

Chesterton was also the first to discuss fully what has come to be thought of as the demonic quality in Dickens's writing and in Dickens himself. The objects in Dickens's novels, he writes, the things which he describes, "he endows with demoniac life. The things seem more actual than things really are." He is referring here to what has recently been understood as the hallucinatory intensity of Dickens's perceptions. Yet he also knows that these hallucinations are not distortions, that "the essence of the good realistic principle . . . is that the most fantastic thing of all is often the precise fact." Chesterton also speaks at length of another side of Dickens's demonic nature, "the primary inexhaustible creative energy, the enormous prodigality of genius." In this connection, he suggests, "one of the godlike things about Dickens is his quantity, his quantity as such, the

enormous output, the incredible fecundity of his invention."
Chesterton is referring to quantity not in the sense that Trollope, with his forty-odd novels, represents quantity, but in the
sense that in fourteen completed novels Dickens created more,
and created more with greater density, than any other English
novelist. It should be noted, however, that the demonic Dickens
of Chesterton is not precisely the same kind of creature as the
demonic Dickens of modern criticism. He is not an unhappy
demon. Chesterton states that Dickens "wanted what a healthy
man wants, only he was ill with wanting it." And what Chesterton says about Quilp applies equally to his vision of Dickens;
"he has a kind of hellish happiness, an atrocious hilarity." Recent comment has concerned itself with the other side of
Dickens, the dark and tortured part of his spirit. Chesterton's
view should not be lost sight of either.

Finally, there is Chesterton's evaluation of Dickens and his
place in literature. In 1906, he stated that Dickens's "place in
nineteenth-century England will not only be high, but altogether
the highest. . . . I venture to offer the proposition that when more
years have passed and more weeding has been effected, Dickens
will dominate the whole England of the nineteenth century; he
will be left on that platform alone." The years have passed, the
weeding has been effected, and Chesterton's judgment has been
substantially verified by the judgment of later generations,
which is only another way of saying the judgment of history.
It was his rare good privilege to have made this judgment,
alone, and at such an early date.

STEVEN MARCUS

Columbia University, New York
January 27, 1965

CHARLES DICKENS

CHAPTER I

THE DICKENS PERIOD

MUCH of our modern difficulty, in religion and other things, arises merely from this: that we confuse the word "indefinable" with the word "vague." If some one speaks of a spiritual fact as "indefinable" we promptly picture something misty, a cloud with indeterminate edges. But this is an error even in commonplace logic. The thing that cannot be defined is the first thing; the primary fact. It is our arms and legs, our pots and pans, that are indefinable. The indefinable is the indisputable. The man next door is indefinable, because he is too actual to be defined. And there are some to whom spiritual things have the same fierce and practical proximity; some to whom God is too actual to be defined.

But there is a third class of primary terms. There are popular expressions which every one

uses and no one can explain; which the wise man
will accept and reverence, as he reverences desire
or darkness or any elemental thing. The prigs
of the debating club will demand that he should
define his terms. And, being a wise man, he will
flatly refuse. This first inexplicable term is the
most important term of all. The word that has
no definition is the word that has no substitute.
If a man falls back again and again on some such
word as "vulgar" or "manly," do not suppose that
the word means nothing because he cannot say
what it means. If he could say what the word
means he would say what it means instead of
saying the word. When the Game Chicken (that
fine thinker) kept on saying to Mr. Toots, "It's
mean. That's what it is—it's mean," he was using
language in the wisest possible way. For what
else could he say? There is no word for mean
except mean. A man must be very mean himself
before he comes to defining meanness. Precisely
because the word is indefinable, the word is
indispensable.

In everyday talk, or in any of our journals, we
may find the loose but important phrase, "Why
have we no great men to-day? Why have we no
great men like Thackeray, or Carlyle, or Dickens?"
Do not let us dismiss this expression, because it

appears loose or arbitrary. "Great" does mean
something, and the test of its actuality is to be
found by noting how instinctively and decisively
we do apply it to some men and not to others;
above all, how instinctively and decisively we do
apply it to four or five men in the Victorian
era, four or five men of whom Dickens was not
the least. The term is found to fit a definite thing.
Whatever the word "great" means, Dickens was
what it means. Even the fastidious and unhappy
who cannot read his books without a continuous
critical exasperation, would use the word of him
without stopping to think. They feel that Dickens
is a great writer even if he is not a good writer.
He is treated as a classic; that is, as a king who
may now be deserted, but who cannot now be
dethroned. The atmosphere of this word clings
to him; and the curious thing is that we cannot
get it to cling to any of the men of our own
generation. "Great" is the first adjective which
the most supercilious modern critic would apply
to Dickens. And "great" is the last adjective that
the most supercilious modern critic would apply
to himself. We dare not claim to be great men,
even when we claim to be superior to them.

Is there, then, any vital meaning in this idea of
"greatness" or in our laments over its absence in

our own time? Some people say, indeed, that this sense of mass is but a mirage of distance, and that men always think dead men great and live men small. They seem to think that the law of perspective in the mental world is the precise opposite to the law of perspective in the physical world. They think that figures grow larger as they walk away. But this theory cannot be made to correspond with the facts. We do not lack great men in our own day because we decline to look for them in our own day; on the contrary, we are looking for them all day long. We are not, as a matter of fact, mere examples of those who stone the prophets and leave it to their posterity to build their sepulchres. If the world would only produce our perfect prophet, solemn, searching, universal, nothing would give us keener pleasure than to build his sepulchre. In our eagerness we might even bury him alive. Nor is it true that the great men of the Victorian era were not called great in their own time. By many they were called great from the first. Charlotte Brontë held this heroic language about Thackeray. Ruskin held it about Carlyle. A definite school regarded Dickens as a great man from the first days of his fame: Dickens certainly belonged to this school.

In reply to this question, "Why have we no

great men to-day?" many modern explanations
are offered. Advertisement, cigarette-smoking, the
decay of religion, the decay of agriculture, too much
humanitarianism, too little humanitarianism, the
fact that people are educated insufficiently, the fact
that they are educated at all, all these are reasons
given. If I give my own explanation, it is not for
its intrinsic value; it is because my answer to the
question, "Why have we no great men?" is a
short way of stating the deepest and most catastro-
phic difference between the age in which we live
and the early nineteenth century; the age under
the shadow of the French Revolution, the age in
which Dickens was born.

The soundest of the Dickens critics, a man of
genius, Mr. George Gissing, opens his criticism by
remarking that the world in which Dickens grew
up was a hard and cruel world. He notes its gross
feeding, its fierce sports, its fighting and foul
humour, and all this he summarizes in the words
hard and cruel. It is curious how different are the
impressions of men. To me this old English world
seems infinitely less hard and cruel than the world
described in Gissing's own novels. Coarse external
customs are merely relative, and easily assimilated.
A man soon learnt to harden his hands and harden
his head. Faced with the world of Gissing, he can

do little but harden his heart.   But the fundamental difference between the beginning of the nineteenth century and the end of it is a difference simple but enormous.   The first period was full of evil things, but it was full of hope.   The second period, the *fin de siécle*, was even full (in some sense) of good things.   But it was occupied in asking what was the good of good things.   Joy itself became joyless; and the fighting of Cobbett was happier than the feasting of Walter Pater.   The men of Cobbett's day were sturdy enough to endure and inflict brutality; but they were also sturdy enough to alter it.   This "hard and cruel" age was, after all, the age of reform.   The gibbet stood up black above them; but it was black against the dawn.

This dawn, against which the gibbet and all the old cruelties stood out so black and clear, was the developing idea of liberalism, the French Revolution.   It was a clear and a happy philosophy.   And only against such philosophies do evils appear evident at all.   The optimist is a better reformer than the pessimist; and the man who believes life to be excellent is the man who alters it most.   It seems a paradox, yet the reason of it is very plain. The pessimist can be enraged at evil.   But only the optimist can be surprised at it.   From the reformer is required a simplicity of surprise.   He

must have the faculty of a violent and virgin
astonishment. It is not enough that he should
think injustice distressing; he must think injustice
absurd, an anomaly in existence, a matter less for
tears than for a shattering laughter. On the other
hand, the pessimists at the end of the century
could hardly curse even the blackest thing; for
they could hardly see it against its black and eternal
background. Nothing was bad, because everything
was bad. Life in prison was infamous—like life
anywhere else. The fires of persecution were vile
—like the stars. We perpetually find this paradox
of a contented discontent. Dr. Johnson takes too
sad a view of humanity, but he is also too satisfied
a Conservative. Rousseau takes too rosy a view of
humanity, but he causes a revolution. Swift is
angry, but a Tory. Shelley is happy, and a rebel.
Dickens, the optimist, satirizes the Fleet, and the
Fleet is gone. Gissing, the pessimist, satirizes
Suburbia, and Suburbia remains.

Mr. Gissing's error, then, about the early
Dickens period we may put thus: in calling it
hard and cruel he omits the wind of hope and
humanity that was blowing through it. It may
have been full of inhuman institutions, but it was
full of humanitarian people. And this humanitarianism was very much the better (in my view)

because it was a rough and even rowdy humanitarianism.   It was free from all the faults that cling
to the name.   It was, if you will, a coarse humanitarianism.   It was a shouting, fighting, drinking
philanthropy—a noble thing.   But, in any case,
this atmosphere was the atmosphere of the
Revolution; and its main idea was the idea of
human equality.   I am not concerned here to defend
the egalitarian idea against the solemn and babyish
attacks made upon it by the rich and learned of
to-day.   I am merely concerned to state one of its
practical consequences.   One of the actual and
certain consequences of the idea that all men are
equal is immediately to produce very great men.
I would say superior men, only that the hero thinks
of himself as great, but not as superior.   This has
been hidden from us of late by a foolish worship of
sinister and exceptional men, men without comradeship, or any infectious virtue.   This type of Cæsar
does exist.   There is a great man who makes every
man feel small.   But the real great man is the man
who makes every man feel great.

The spirit of the early century produced great
men, because it believed that men were great.   It
made strong men by encouraging weak men.   Its
education, its public habits, its rhetoric, were all
addressed towards encouraging the greatness in

everybody. And by encouraging the greatness in everybody, it naturally encouraged superlative greatness in some. Superiority came out of the high rapture of equality. It is precisely in this sort of passionate unconsciousness and bewildering community of thought that men do become more than themselves. No man by taking thought can add one cubit to his stature; but a man may add many cubits to his stature by not taking thought. The best men of the Revolution were simply common men at their best. This is why our age can never understand Napoleon. Because he was something great and triumphant, we suppose that he must have been something extraordinary, something inhuman. Some say he was the Devil; some say he was the Superman. Was he a very, very bad man? Was he a good man with some greater moral code? We strive in vain to invent the mysteries behind that immortal mask of brass. The modern world with all its subtleness will never guess his strange secret; for his strange secret was that he was very like other people.

And almost without exception all the great men have come out of this atmosphere of equality. Great men may make despotisms; but democracies make great men. The other main factory of heroes besides a revolution is a religion. And a religion again, is a thing which, by its nature, does not think of men as more or less valuable, but of men as all intensely and painfully valuable, a democracy of eternal danger. For religion all men are equal, as all pennies are equal, because the only value in any of them is that they bear the image of the King. This fact has been quite insufficiently observed in the study of religious heroes. Piety produces intellectual greatness precisely because piety in itself is quite indifferent to intellectual greatness. The strength of Cromwell was that he cared for religion. But the strength of religion was that it did not care for Cromwell; did not care for him, that is, any more than for anybody else. He and his footman were equally welcomed to warm places in the hospitality of hell. It has often been said, very truly, that religion is the thing that makes the ordinary man feel extra-ordinary; it is an equally important truth that religion is the thing that makes the extraordinary man feel ordinary.

Carlyle killed the heroes; there have been none since his time. He killed the heroic (which he sincerely loved) by forcing upon each man this question: "Am I strong or weak?" To which the answer from any honest man whatever (yes, from Cæsar or Bismarck) would certainly be "weak." He asked for candidates for a definite aristocracy, for men who should hold themselves consciously above their fellows. He advertised for them, so to speak; he promised them glory; he promised them omnipotence. They have not appeared yet. They never will. For the real heroes of whom he wrote had appeared out of an ecstacy of the ordinary. I have already instanced such a case as Cromwell. But there is no need to go through all the great men of Carlyle. Carlyle himself was as great as any of them; and if ever there was a typical child of the French Revolution, it was he. He began with the wildest hopes from the Reform Bill, and although he soured afterwards, he had been made and moulded by those hopes. He was disappointed with Equality; but Equality was not disappointed with him. Equality is justified of all her children.

But we, in the post-Carlylean period, have become fastidious about great men. Every man examines himself, every man examines his neighbours, to see whether they or he quite come up to the exact line of greatness. The answer is, naturally, "No." And many a man calls himself contentedly "a minor poet" who would then have been inspired to be a major prophet. We are hard to please and of little faith. We can hardly believe that there is such a thing as a great man. They could hardly believe there was such a thing as a small one. But we are always praying that our eyes may behold greatness, instead of praying that our hearts may be filled with it. Thus, for instance, the Liberal party (to which I belong) was, in its period of exile, always saying, "O for a Gladstone!" and such things. We were always asking that it might be strengthened from above, instead of ourselves strengthening it from below, with our hope and our anger and our youth. Every man was waiting for a leader. Every man ought to be waiting for a chance to lead. If a god does come upon the earth, he will descend at the sight of the brave. Our prostrations and litanies are of no avail; our new moons and our sabbaths are an abomination. The great man will come when all of us are feeling great, not when all of us are feeling small. He will ride in at some splendid moment when we all feel that we could do without him.

We are then able to answer in some manner the question, "Why have we no great men?" We have no great men chiefly because we are always looking for them. We are connoisseurs of greatness, and connoisseurs can never be great; we are fastidious, that is, we are small. When Diogenes went about with a lantern looking for an honest man, I am afraid he had very little time to be honest himself. And when anybody goes about on his hands and knees looking for a great man to worship, he is making sure that one man at any rate shall not be great. Now, the error of Diogenes is evident. The error of Diogenes lay in the fact that he omitted to notice that every man is both an honest man and a dishonest man. Diogenes looked for his honest man inside every crypt and cavern; but he never thought of looking inside the thief. And that is where the Founder of Christianity found the honest man; He found him on a gibbet and promised him Paradise. Just as Christianity looked for the honest man inside the thief, democracy looked for the wise man inside the fool. It encouraged the fool to be wise. We can call this thing sometimes optimism, sometimes equality; the nearest name for it is encouragement. It had its exaggerations—failure to understand original sin, notions that education would make all men good, the childlike yet pedantic philosophies of human perfectibility. But the whole was full of a faith in the infinity of human souls, which is in itself not only Christian but orthodox; and this we have lost amid the limitations of a pessimistic science. Christianity said that any man could be

a saint if he chose; democracy, that any man could
be a citizen if he chose. The note of the last few
decades in art and ethics has been that a man is
stamped with an irrevocable psychology, and is
cramped for perpetuity in the prison of his skull.
It was a world that expected everything of everybody. It was a world that encouraged anybody
to be anything. And in England and literature
its living expression was Dickens.

We shall consider Dickens in many other
capacities, but let us put this one first. He was
the voice in England of this humane intoxication
and expansion, this encouraging of anybody to be
anything. His best books are a carnival of liberty,
and there is more of the real spirit of the French
Revolution in "Nicholas Nickleby" than in "The
Tale of Two Cities." His work has the great glory
of the Revolution, the bidding of every man to be
himself; it has also the revolutionary deficiency:
it seems to think that this mere emancipation is
enough. No man *encouraged* his characters so
much as Dickens. "I am an affectionate father,"
he says, "to every child of my fancy." He was
not only an affectionate father, he was an over-
indulgent father. The children of his fancy are
spoilt children. They shake the house like heavy
and shouting schoolboys; they smash the story to

pieces like so much furniture. When we moderns write stories our characters are better controlled. But, alas! our characters are rather easier to control. We are in no danger from the gigantic gambols of creatures like Mantalini and Micawber. We are in no danger of giving our readers too much Weller or Wegg. We have not got it to give. When we experience the ungovernable sense of life which goes along with the old Dickens sense of liberty, we experience the best of the revolution. We are filled with the first of all democratic doctrines, that all men are interesting; Dickens tried to make some of his people appear dull people, but he could not keep them dull. He could not make a monotonous man. The bores in his books are brighter than the wits in other books.

I have put this position first for a defined reason. It is useless for us to attempt to imagine Dickens and his life unless we are able at least to imagine this old atmosphere of a democratic optimism—a confidence in common men. Dickens depends upon such a comprehension in a rather unusual manner, a manner worth explanation, or at least remark.

The disadvantage under which Dickens has fallen, both as an artist and a moralist, is very plain. His misfortune is that neither of the two last movements in literary criticism has done him any good. He has suffered alike from his enemies, and from the enemies of his enemies. The facts to which I refer are familiar. When the world first awoke from the mere hypnotism of Dickens, from the direct tyranny of his temperament, there was, of course, a reaction. At the head of it came the Realists, with their documents, like Miss Flite. They declared that scenes and types in Dickens were wholly impossible (in which they were perfectly right), and on this rather paradoxical ground objected to them as literature. They were not "like life," and there, they thought, was an end of the matter. The realist for a time prevailed. But Realists did not enjoy their victory (if they enjoyed anything) very long. A more symbolic school of criticism soon arose. Men saw that it was necessary to give a much deeper and more delicate meaning to the expression "like life." Streets are not life, cities and civilizations are not life, faces even and voices are not life itself. Life is within, and no man hath seen it at any time. As for our meals, and our manners, and our daily dress, these are things exactly like sonnets; they are random symbols of the soul. One man tries to express himself in books, another in boots; both probably fail. Our solid houses and square meals are in the

strict sense fiction. They are things made up to
typify our thoughts. The coat a man wears may
be wholly fictitious; the movement of his hands
may be quite unlike life.

This much the intelligence of men soon perceived. And by this much Dickens's fame should
have greatly profited. For Dickens is " like life "
in the truer sense, in the sense that he is akin to
the living principle in us and in the universe; he is
like life, at least in this detail, that he is alive.
His art is like life, because, like life, it cares for
nothing outside itself, and goes on its way rejoicing.
Both produce monsters with a kind of carelessness, like enormous by-products; life producing
the rhinoceros, and art Mr. Bunsby. Art indeed
copies life in not copying life, for life copies
nothing. Dickens's art is like life because, like
life, it is irresponsible, because, like life, it is
incredible.

Yet the return of this realization has not greatly
profited Dickens, the return of romance has been
almost useless to this great romantic. He has
gained as little from the fall of the realists as
from their triumph; there has been a revolution,
there has been a counter revolution, there has been
no restoration. And the reason of this brings us
back to that atmosphere of popular optimism of

which I spoke. And the shortest way of expressing the more recent neglect of Dickens is to say
that for our time and taste he exaggerates the
wrong thing.

Exaggeration is the definition of art. That both
Dickens and the Moderns understood. Art is, in
its inmost nature, fantastic. Time brings queer re-
venges, and while the realists were yet living, the
art of Dickens was justified by Aubrey Beardsley.
But men like Aubrey Beardsley were allowed to
be fantastic, because the mood which they overstrained and overstated was a mood which their
period understood. Dickens overstrains and over-
states a mood our period does not understand.
The truth he exaggerates is exactly this old Revolution sense of infinite opportunity and boisterous
brotherhood. And we resent his undue sense of
it, because we ourselves have not even a due sense
of it. We feel troubled with too much where we
have too little; we wish he would keep it within
bounds. For we are all exact and scientific on the
subjects we do not care about. We all immediately
detect exaggeration in an exposition of Mormonism
or a patriotic speech from Paraguay. We all require sobriety on the subject of the sea-serpent.
But the moment we begin to believe a thing ourselves, that moment we begin easily to overstate

it ; and the moment our souls become serious, our words become a little wild. And certain moderns are thus placed towards exaggeration. They permit any writer to emphasize doubts for instance, for doubts are their religion, but they permit no man to emphasize dogmas. If a man be the mildest Christian, they smell "cant ;" but he can be a raving windmill of pessimism, "and they call it "temperament." If a moralist paints a wild picture of immorality, they doubt its truth, they say that devils are not so black as they are painted. But if a pessimist paints a wild picture of melancholy, they accept the whole horrible psychology, and they never ask if devils are as blue as they are painted.

It is evident, in short, why even those who admire exaggeration do not admire Dickens. He is exaggerating the wrong thing. They know what it is to feel a sadness so strange and deep that only impossible characters can express it : they do not know what it is to feel a joy so vital and violent that only impossible characters can express that. They know that the soul can be so sad as to dream naturally of the blue faces of the corpses of Baudelaire : they do not know that the soul can be so cheerful as to dream naturally of the blue face of Major Bagstock. They know that there is a point of depression at which one believes in Tintagiles : they do not know that there is a point of exhilaration at which one believes in Mr. Wegg. To them the impossibilities of Dickens seem much more impossible than they really are, because they are already attuned to the opposite impossibilities of Maeterlinck. For every mood there is an appropriate impossibility—a decent and tactful impossibility—fitted to the frame of mind. Every train of thought may end in an ecstasy, and all roads lead to Elfland. But few now walk far enough along the street of Dickens to find the place where the cockney villas grow so comic that they become poetical. People do not know how far mere good spirits will go. For instance, we never think (as the old folk-lore did) of good spirits reaching to the spiritual world. We see this in the complete absence from modern, popular supernaturalism of the old popular mirth. We hear plenty to-day of the wisdom of the spiritual world ; but we do not hear, as our fathers did, of the folly of the spiritual world, of the tricks of the gods, and the jokes of the patron saints. Our popular tales tell us of a man who is so wise that he touches the supernatural, like Dr. Nikola ; but they never tell us (like the popular tales of the past) of a man who was so silly that he touched the supernatural, like

Bottom the Weaver. We do not understand the dark and transcendental sympathy between fairies and fools. We understand a devout occultism, an evil occultism, a tragic occultism, but a farcical occultism is beyond us. Yet a farcical occultism is the very essence of "The Midsummer Night's Dream." It is also the right and credible essence of " The Christmas Carol." Whether we understand it depends upon whether we can understand that exhilaration is not a physical accident, but a mystical fact; that exhilaration can be infinite, like sorrow; that a joke can be so big that it breaks the roof of the stars. By simply going on being absurd, a thing can become godlike; there is but one step from the ridiculous to the sublime.

Dickens was great because he was immoderately possessed with all this; if we are to understand him at all we must also be moderately possessed with it. We must understand this old limitless hilarity and human confidence, at least enough to be able to endure it when it is pushed a great deal too far. For Dickens did push it too far; he did push the hilarity to the point of incredible character-drawing; he did push the human confidence to the point of an unconvincing sentimentalism. You can trace, if you will, the revolutionary joy till it reaches the incredible Sapsea epitaph; you can trace the

revolutionary hope till it reaches the repentance
of Dombey. There is plenty to carp at in this
man if you are inclined to carp; you may easily
find him vulgar if you cannot see that he is divine;
and if you cannot laugh with Dickens, undoubtedly
you can laugh at him.

I believe myself that this braver world of his
will certainly return; for I believe that it is bound
up with the realities, like morning and the spring.
But for those who beyond remedy regard it as an
error, I put this appeal before any other observa-
tions on Dickens. First let us sympathize, if only
for an instant, with the hopes of the Dickens period,
with that cheerful trouble of change. If democracy
has disappointed you, do not think of it as a burst
bubble, but at least as a broken heart, an old love-
affair. Do not sneer at the time when the creed of
humanity was on its honeymoon; treat it with the
dreadful reverence that is due to youth. For you,
perhaps, a drearier philosophy has covered and
eclipsed the earth. The fierce poet of the Middle
Ages wrote, "Abandon hope, all ye who enter
here," over the gates of the lower world. The
emancipated poets of to-day have written it over
the gates of this world. But if we are to understand the story which follows, we must erase that
apocalyptic writing, if only for an hour. We must

recreate the faith of our fathers, if only as an artistic atmosphere. If, then, you are a pessimist, in reading this story, forego for a little the pleasures of pessimism. Dream for one mad moment that the grass is green. Unlearn that sinister learning that you think so clear; deny that deadly knowledge that you think you know. Surrender the very flower of your culture; give up the very jewel of your pride; abandon hopelessness, all ye who enter here.

CHAPTER II

THE BOYHOOD OF DICKENS

CHARLES DICKENS was born at Landport, in Portsea, on February 7, 1812. His father was a clerk in the Navy Pay-office, and was temporarily on duty in the neighbourhood. Very soon after the birth of Charles Dickens, however, the family moved for a short period to Norfolk Street, Bloomsbury, and then for a long period to Chatham, which thus became the real home, and for all serious purposes, the native place of Dickens. The whole story of his life moves like a Canterbury pilgrimage along the great roads of Kent.

John Dickens, his father, was, as stated, a clerk; but such mere terms of trade tell us little of the tone or status of a family. Browning's father (to take an instance at random) would also be described as a clerk and a man of the middle class; but the Browning family and the Dickens family have the colour of two different civilizations. The difference cannot be conveyed merely by saying that Browning stood many strata above Dickens. It must also be conveyed that Browning belonged to that section of the middle class which tends (in the small social sense) to rise; the Dickenses to that section which tends in the same sense to fall. If Browning had not been a poet, he would have been a better clerk than his father, and his son probably a better and richer clerk than he. But if they had not been lifted in the air by the enormous accident of a man of genius, the Dickenses, I fancy, would have appeared in poorer and poorer places, as inventory clerks, as caretakers, as addressers of envelopes, until they melted into the masses of the poor.

Yet at the time of Dickens's birth and childhood this weakness in their worldly destiny was in no way apparent; especially it was not apparent to the little Charles himself. He was born and grew up in a paradise of small prosperity. He fell into the family, so to speak, during one of its comfortable periods, and he never in those early days thought of himself as anything but as a comfortable middle-class child, the son of a comfortable middle-class man. The father whom he found provided for him, was one from whom comfort drew forth his most pleasant and reassuring qualities, though not perhaps his most interesting and peculiar. John Dickens seemed, most probably, a hearty and kindly character, a little florid of speech, a little careless of duty in some details, notably in the detail of education. His neglect of his son's mental training in later and more trying times was a piece of unconscious selfishness which remained a little acrimoniously in his son's mind through life. But even in this earlier and easier period what records there are of John Dickens give out the air of a somewhat idle and irresponsible fatherhood. He exhibited towards his son that contradiction in conduct which is always shown by the too thoughtless parent to the too thoughtful child. He contrived at once to neglect his mind, and also to over-stimulate it.

There are many recorded tales and traits of the author's infancy, but one small fact seems to me more than any other to strike the note and give the key to his whole strange character. His father found it more amusing to be an audience than to be an instructor; and instead of giving the child intellectual pleasure, called upon him, almost before he was out of petticoats, to provide it. Some of the earliest glimpses we have of Charles Dickens show him to us perched on some chair or table singing comic songs in an atmosphere of perpetual applause. So, almost as soon as he can toddle, he steps into the glare of the footlights. He never stepped out of it until he died. He was a good man, as men go in this bewildering world of ours, brave, transparent, tender-hearted, scrupulously independent and honourable; he was not a man whose weaknesses should be spoken of without some delicacy and doubt. But there did mingle with his merits all his life this theatrical quality, this atmosphere of being shown off—a sort of hilarious self-consciousness. His literary life was a triumphal procession; he died drunken with glory. And behind all this nine years' wonder that filled the world, behind his gigantic tours and his ten thousand editions, the crowded lectures and the crashing brass, behind all the thing we really see is the flushed face of a little boy singing music-hall songs to a circle of aunts and uncles. And this precocious pleasure explains much, too, in the moral way. Dickens had all his life the faults of the little boy who is kept up too late at night. The boy in such a case exhibits a psychological paradox; he is a little too irritable because he is a little too happy. Dickens was always a little too irritable because he was a little too happy. Like the over-wrought child in society, he was splendidly sociable, and yet suddenly quarrelsome. In all the practical relations of his life he was what the child is in the last hours of an evening party, genuinely delighted, genuinely delightful, genuinely affectionate and happy, and yet in some strange way fundamentally exasperated and dangerously close to tears.

There was another touch about the boy which made his case more peculiar, and perhaps his intelligence more fervid; the touch of ill-health. It could not be called more than a touch, for he suffered from no formidable malady and could always through life endure a great degree of exertion, even if it was only the exertion of walking violently all night. Still the streak of sickness was sufficient to take him out of the common unconscious life of the community of boys; and for good or evil that withdrawal is always a matter of deadly importance to the mind. He was thrown back perpetually upon the pleasures of the intelligence, and these began to burn in his head like a pent and painful furnace. In his own unvaryingly vivid way he has described how he crawled up into an unconsidered garret, and there found, in a dusty heap, the undying literature of England. The books he mentions chiefly are "Humphry Clinker" and "Tom Jones." When he opened those two books in the garret he caught hold of the only past with which he is at all connected, the great comic writers of England of whom he was destined to be the last.

It must be remembered (as I have suggested before) that there was something about the county in which he lived, and the great roads along which he travelled that sympathized with and stimulated his pleasure in this old picaresque literature. The groups that came along the road, that passed through his town and out of it, were of the motley laughable type that tumbled into ditches or beat down the doors of taverns under the escort of Smollett and Fielding. In our time the main roads of Kent have upon them very often a perpetual procession of tramps and tinkers unknown on the quiet hills of Sussex; and it may have been so also in Dickens's boyhood. In his neighbourhood were definite memorials of yet older and yet greater English comedy. From the height of Gads-hill at which he stared unceasingly there looked down upon him the monstrous ghost of Falstaff, Falstaff who might well have been the spiritual father of all Dickens's adorable knaves, Falstaff the great mountain of English laughter and English senti- mentalism, the great, healthy, humane English humbug, not to be matched among the nations.

At this eminence of Gads-hill Dickens used to stare even as a boy with the steady purpose of some day making it his own. It is characteristic of the consistency which underlies the superficially

erratic career of Dickens that he actually did live
to make it his own. The truth is that he was a
precocious child, precocious not only on the more
poetical but on the more prosaic side of life. He
was ambitious as well as enthusiastic. No one can
ever know what visions they were that crowded
into the head of the clever little brat as he ran
about the streets of Chatham or stood glowering
at Gads-hill. But I think that quite mundane
visions had a very considerable share in the matter.
He longed to go to school (a strange wish), to go
to college, to make a name, nor did he merely
aspire to these things; the great number of them
he also expected. He regarded himself as a child
of good position just about to enter on a life of
good luck. He thought his home and family a
very good spring-board or jumping-off place from
which to fling himself to the positions which he
desired to reach. And almost as he was about
to spring the whole structure broke under him,
and he and all that belonged to him disappeared
into a darkness far below.

Everything had been struck down as with the
finality of a thunder-bolt. His lordly father was
a bankrupt, and in the Marshalsea prison. His
mother was in a mean home in the north of
London, wildly proclaiming herself the principal

of a girl's school, a girl's school to which nobody would go. And he himself, the conqueror of the world and the prospective purchaser of Gads-hill, passed some distracted and bewildering days in pawning the household necessities to Fagins in foul shops, and then found himself somehow or other one of a row of ragged boys in a great dreary factory, pasting the same kinds of labels on to the same kinds of blacking-bottles from morning till night.

Although it seemed sudden enough to him, the disintegration had, as a matter of fact, of course, been going on for a long time. He had only heard from his father dark and melodramatic allusions to a "deed" which, from the way it was mentioned, might have been a claim to the crown or a compact with the devil, but which was in truth an unsuccessful documentary attempt on the part of John Dickens to come to a composition with his creditors. And now, in the lurid light of his sunset, the character of John Dickens began to take on those purple colours which have made him under another name absurd and immortal. It required a tragedy to bring out this man's comedy. So long as John Dickens was in easy circumstances, he seemed only an easy man, a little long and luxuriant in his phrases, a little

careless in his business routine. He seemed only
a wordy man, who lived on bread and beef like
his neighbours; but as bread and beef were
successively taken away from him, it was discovered that he lived on words. For him to be
involved in a calamity only meant to be cast for
the first part in a tragedy. For him blank ruin
was only a subject for blank verse. Henceforth
we feel scarcely inclined to call him John Dickens
at all; we feel inclined to call him by the name
through which his son celebrated this preposterous
and sublime victory of the human spirit over circumstances. Dickens, in "David Copperfield,"
called him Wilkins Micawber. In his personal
correspondence he called him the Prodigal Father.

Young Charles had been hurriedly flung into the
factory by the more or less careless good-nature
of James Lamert, a relation of his mother's; it
was a blacking factory, supposed to be run as a
rival to Warren's by another and "original"
Warren, both practically conducted by another of
the Lamerts. It was situated near Hungerford
Market. Dickens worked there drearily, like one
stunned with disappointment. To a child excessively intellectualized, and at this time, I fear,
excessively egotistical, the coarseness of the whole
thing—the work, the rooms, the boys, the language

—was a sort of bestial nightmare. Not only did he scarcely speak of it then, but he scarcely spoke of it afterwards. Years later, in the fulness of his fame, he heard from Forster that a man had spoken of knowing him. On hearing the name, he somewhat curtly acknowledged it, and spoke of having seen the man once. Forster, in his innocence, answered that the man said he had seen Dickens many times in a factory by Hungerford Market. Dickens was suddenly struck with a long and extraordinary silence. Then he invited Forster, as his best friend, to a particular interview, and, with every appearance of difficulty and distress, told him the whole story for the first and the last time. A long while after that he told the world some part of the matter in the account of Murdstone and Grinby's in " David Copperfield." He never spoke of the whole experience except once or twice, and he never spoke of it otherwise than as a man might speak of hell.

It need not be suggested, I think, that this agony in the child was exaggerated by the man. It is true that he was not incapable of the vice of exaggeration, if it be a vice. There was about him much vanity and a certain virulence in his version of many things. Upon the whole, indeed, it would hardly be too much to say that he would

have exaggerated any sorrow he talked about.
But this was a sorrow with a very strange position
in Dickens's life; it was a sorrow he did not talk
about. Upon this particular dark spot he kept a
sort of deadly silence for twenty years. An
accident revealed part of the truth to the dearest
of all his friends. He then told the whole truth
to the dearest of all his friends. He never told
anybody else. I do not think that this arose from
any social sense of disgrace; if he had it slightly
at the time, he was far too self-satisfied a man to
have taken it seriously in after life. I really think
that his pain at this time was so real and ugly that
the thought of it filled him with that sort of impersonal but unbearable shame with which we
are filled, for instance, by the notion of physical
torture, of something that humiliates humanity.
He felt that such agony was something obscene.
Moreover there are two other good reasons for
thinking that his sense of hopelessness was very
genuine. First of all, this starless outlook is
common in the calamities of boyhood. The bitterness of boyish distresses does not lie in the fact
that they are large; it lies in the fact that we do
not know that they are small. About any early
disaster there is a dreadful finality; a lost child can
suffer like a lost soul.

It is currently said that hope goes with youth,
and lends to youth its wings of a butterfly; but
I fancy that hope is the last gift given to man, and
the only gift not given to youth. Youth is pre-
eminently the period in which a man can be lyric,
fanatical, poetic; but youth is the period in which
a man can be hopeless. The end of every episode
is the end of the world. But the power of hoping
through everything, the knowledge that the soul
survives its adventures, that great inspiration
comes to the middle-aged; God has kept that good
wine until now. It is from the backs of the elderly
gentlemen that the wings of the butterfly should
burst. There is nothing that so much mystifies
the young as the consistent frivolity of the old.
They have discovered their indestructibility. They
are in their second and clearer childhood, and there
is a meaning in the merriment of their eyes. They
have seen the end of the End of the World.

First, then, the desolate finality of Dickens's
childish mood makes me think it was a real one.
And there is another thing to be remembered.
Dickens, was not a saintly child after the style
of Little Dorrit or Little Nell. He had not, at
this time at any rate, set his heart wholly upon
higher things, even upon things such as personal
tenderness or loyalty. He had been, and was,

unless I am very much mistaken, sincerely, stubbornly, bitterly ambitious.   He had, I fancy, a
fairly clear idea previous to the downfall of all
his family's hopes of what he wanted to do in the
world, and of the mark that he meant to make
there.   In no dishonourable sense, but still in a
definite sense, he might, in early life, be called
worldly; and the children of this world are in
their generation infinitely more sensitive than the
children of light.   A saint after repentance will
forgive himself for a sin; a man about town will
never forgive himself for a *faux pas.*   There are
ways of getting absolved for murder; there are no
ways of getting absolved for upsetting the soup.
This thin-skinned quality in all very mundane
people is a thing too little remembered; and it
must not be wholly forgotten in connection with
a clever, restless lad who dreamed of a destiny.
That part of his distress which concerned himself
and his social standing was among the other parts
of it the least noble; but perhaps it was the most
painful.   For pride is not only, as the modern world
fails to understand, a sin to be condemned; it is
also (as it understands even less) a weakness to be
very much commiserated.   A very vitalizing touch
is given in one of his own reminiscences.   His
most unendurable moment did not come in any

bullying in the factory or any famine in the streets. It came when he went to see his sister Fanny take a prize at the Royal Academy of Music. " I could not bear to think of myself—beyond the reach of all such honourable emulation and success. The tears ran down my face. I felt as if my heart were rent. I prayed when I went to bed that night to be lifted out of the humiliation and neglect in which I was. I never had suffered so much before. There was no envy in this." I do not think that there was, though the poor little wretch could hardly have been blamed if there had been. There was only a furious sense of frustration; a spirit like a wild beast in a cage. It was only a small matter in the external and obvious sense; it was only Dickens prevented from being Dickens.

If we put these facts together, that the tragedy seemed final, and that the tragedy was concerned with the supersensitive matters of the ego and the gentleman, I think we can imagine a pretty genuine case of internal depression. And when we add to the case of the internal depression the case of the external oppression, the case of the material circumstances by which he was surrounded, we have reached a sort of midnight. All day he worked on insufficient food at a factory. It is sufficient to say that it afterwards appeared in his

works as Murdstone and Grinby's. At night he
returned disconsolately to a lodging-house for such
lads, kept by an old lady. It is sufficient to say
that she appeared afterwards as Mrs. Pipchin.
Once a week only he saw anybody for whom he
cared a straw; that was when he went to the
Marshalsea prison, and that gave his juvenile
pride, half manly and half snobbish, bitter annoy-
ance of another kind. Add to this, finally, that
physically he was always very weak and never
very well. Once he was struck down in the middle
of his work with sudden bodily pain. The boy
who worked next to him, a coarse and heavy lad
named Bob Fagin, who had often attacked Dickens
on the not unreasonable ground of his being a
"gentleman," suddenly showed that enduring sanity
of compassion which Dickens had destined to show
so often in the characters of the common and un-
clean. Fagin made a bed for his sick companion
out of the straw in the workroom, and filled empty
blacking bottles with hot water all day. When the
evening came, and Dickens was somewhat recovered, Bob Fagin insisted on escorting the boy
home to his father. The situation was as poignant
as a sort of tragic farce. Fagin in his wooden-
headed chivalry would have died in order to take
Dickens to his family; Dickens in his bitter gentility

would have died rather than let Fagin know that his family were in the Marshalsea. So these two young idiots tramped the tedious streets, both stubborn, both suffering for an idea. The advantage certainly was with Fagin, who was suffering for a Christian compassion, while Dickens was suffering for a pagan pride. At last Dickens flung off his friend with desperate farewell and thanks, and dashed up the steps of a strange house on the Surrey side. He knocked and rang as Bob Fagin, his benefactor and his incubus, disappeared round the corner. And when the servant came to open the door, he asked, apparently with gravity, whether Mr. Robert Fagin lived there. It is a strange touch. The immortal Dickens woke in him for an instant in that last wild joke of that weary evening. Next morning, however, he was again well enough to make himself ill again, and the wheels of the great factory went on. They manufactured a number of bottles of Warren's Blacking, and in the course of the process they manufactured also the greatest optimist of the nineteenth century.

This boy who dropped down groaning at his work, who was hungry four or five times a week, whose best feelings and worst feelings were alike flayed alive, was the man on whom two

generations of comfortable critics have visited
the complaint that his view of life was too
rosy to be anything but unreal. Afterwards,
and in its proper place, I shall speak of what
is called the optimism of Dickens, and of whether
it was really too cheerful or too smooth. But
this boyhood of his may be recorded now as a
mere fact. If he was too happy, this was where
he learnt it. If his school of thought was a vulgar
optimism, this is where he went to school. If he
learnt to whitewash the universe, it was in a
blacking factory that he learnt it.

As a fact, there is no shred of evidence to show
that those who have had sad experiences tend to
have a sad philosophy. There are numberless
points upon which Dickens is spiritually at one
with the poor, that is, with the great mass of mankind. But there is no point in which he is more
perfectly at one with them than in showing that
there is no kind of connection between a man being
unhappy and a man being pessimistic. Sorrow and
pessimism are indeed, in a sense, opposite things,
since sorrow is founded on the value of something, and pessimism upon the value of nothing.
And in practice we find that those poets or
political leaders who come from the people, and
whose experiences have really been searching and

cruel, are the most sanguine people in the world. These men out of the old agony are always optimists; they are sometimes offensive optimists. A man like Robert Burns, whose father (like Dickens' father) goes bankrupt, whose whole life is a struggle against miserable external powers and internal weaknesses yet more miserable—a man whose life begins grey and ends black—Burns does not merely sing about the goodness of life, he positively rants and cants about it. Rousseau, whom all his friends and acquaintances treated almost as badly as he treated them—Rousseau does not grow merely eloquent, he grows gushing and sentimental, about the inherent goodness of human nature. Charles Dickens, who was most miserable at the receptive age when most people are most happy, is afterwards happy when all men weep. Circumstances break men's bones; it has never been shown that they break men's optimism. These great popular leaders do all kinds of desperate things under the immediate scourge of tragedy. They become drunkards; they become demagogues; they become morpho-maniacs. They never become pessimists. Most unquestionably there are ragged and unhappy men whom we could easily understand being pessimists. But as a matter of fact they are not pessimists. Most unquestionably there are whole dim hordes of humanity whom we should promptly pardon if they cursed God. But they don't. The pessimists are aristocrats like Byron; the men who curse God are aristocrats like Swinburne. But when those who starve and suffer speak for a moment, they do not profess merely an optimism, they profess a cheap optimism; they are too poor to afford a dear one. They cannot indulge in any detailed or merely logical defence of life; that would be to delay the enjoyment of it. These higher optimists, of whom Dickens was one, do not approve of the universe; they do not even admire the universe; they fall in love with it. They embrace life too close to criticize or even to see it. Existence to such men has the wild beauty of a woman, and those love her with most intensity who love her with least cause.

CHAPTER III

THE YOUTH OF DICKENS

THERE are popular phrases so picturesque that even when they are intentionally funny they are unintentionally poetical. I remember, to take one instance out of many, hearing a heated Secularist in Hyde Park apply to some parson or other the exquisite expression, "a sky-pilot." Subsequent inquiry has taught me that the term is intended to be comic and even contemptuous; but in that first freshness of it I went home repeating it to myself like a new poem. Few of the pious legends have conceived so strange and yet celestial a picture as this of the pilot in the sky, leaning on his helm above the empty heavens, and carrying his cargo of souls higher than the loneliest cloud. The phrase is like a lyric of Shelley. Or, to take another instance from another language, the French have an incomparable idiom for a boy playing truant: "Il fait l'école buissonnière"—he goes to the bushy school, or the school among the bushes. How admirably this accidental expression, "the bushy school" (not to be lightly confounded with

the Art School at Bushey)—how admirably this
"bushy school" expresses half the modern notions
of a more natural education! The two words
express the whole poetry of Wordsworth, the
whole philosophy of Thoreau, and are quite as
good literature as either.

Now, among a million of such scraps of inspired
slang there is one which describes a certain side of
Dickens better than pages of explanation. The
phrase, appropriately enough, occurs at least once
in his works, and that on a fitting occasion. When
Job Trotter is sent by Sam on a wild chase after
Mr. Perker, the solicitor, Mr. Perker's clerk con-
doles with Job upon the lateness of the hour, and
the fact that all habitable places are shut up. "My
friend," says Mr. Perker's clerk, "you've got the
key of the street." Mr. Perker's clerk, who was a
flippant and scornful young man, may perhaps be
pardoned if he used this expression in a flippant
and scornful sense; but let us hope that Dickens
did not. Let us hope that Dickens saw the strange,
yet satisfying, imaginative justice of the words;
for Dickens himself had, in the most sacred and
serious sense of the term, the key of the street.
When we shut out anything, we are shut out of
that thing. When we shut out the street, we are
shut out of the street. Few of us understand the

street. Even when we step into it, we step into it doubtfully, as into a house or room of strangers. Few of us see through the shining riddle of the street, the strange folk that belong to the street only—the street-walker or the street arab, the nomads who, generation after generation, have kept their ancient secrets in the full blaze of the sun. Of the street at night many of us know even less. The street at night is a great house locked up. But Dickens had, if ever man had, the key of the street. His earth was the stones of the street; his stars were the lamps of the street; his hero was the man in the street. He could open the inmost door of his house—the door that leads into that secret passage which is lined with houses and roofed with stars.

This silent transformation into a citizen of the street took place during those dark days of boyhood, when Dickens was drudging at the factory. Whenever he had done drudging, he had no other resource but drifting, and he drifted over half London. He was a dreamy child, thinking mostly of his own dreary prospects. Yet he saw and remembered much of the streets and squares he passed. Indeed, as a matter of fact, he went the right way to work unconsciously to do so. He did not go in for " observation," a priggish habit;

he did not look at Charing Cross to improve his
mind or count the lamp-posts in Holborn to
practise his arithmetic. But unconsciously he made
all these places the scenes of the monstrous drama
in his miserable little soul. He walked in darkness
under the lamps of Holborn, and was crucified at
Charing Cross. So for him ever afterwards these
places had the beauty that only belongs to battle-
fields. For our memory never fixes the facts which
we have merely observed. The only way to remember a place for ever is to live in the place for
an hour; and the only way to live in the place for
an hour is to forget the place for an hour. The
undying scenes we can all see if we shut our eyes
are not the scenes that we have stared at under the
direction of guide-books; the scenes we see are the
scenes at which we did not look at all—the scenes
in which we walked when we were thinking about
something else—about a sin, or a love-affair, or
some childish sorrow. We can see the background
now because we did not see it then. So Dickens
did not stamp these places on his mind; he stamped
his mind on these places. For him ever afterwards
these streets were mortally romantic; they were
dipped in the purple dyes of youth and its tragedy,
and rich with irrevocable sunsets.

Herein is the whole secret of that eerie realism

with which Dickens could always vitalize some
dark or dull corner of London.   There are details
in the Dickens' descriptions—a window, or a
railing, or the keyhole of a door—which he endows
with demoniac life.   The things seem more actual
than things really are.   Indeed, that degree of
realism does not exist in reality : it is the unbearable realism of a dream.   And this kind of realism
can only be gained by walking dreamily in a place ;
it cannot be gained by walking observantly.
Dickens himself has given a perfect instance of
how these nightmare minutiæ grew upon him in
his trance of abstraction.   He mentions among the
coffee-shops into which he crept in those wretched
days in St. Martin's Lane, "of which I only
recollect that it stood near the church, and that
in the door there was an oval glass plate with
'COFFEE ROOM' painted on it, addressed to
wards the street.   If I ever find myself in a very
different kind of coffee-room now, but where there
is such an inscription on glass, and read it back-
wards on the wrong side, MOOR EEFFOC (as I
often used to do then in a dismal reverie), a shock
goes through my blood."   That wild word, "Moor
Eeffoc," is the motto of all effective realism ; it is
the masterpiece of the good realistic principle—the
principle that the most fantastic thing of all is often

the precise fact. And that elvish kind of realism Dickens adopted everywhere. His world was alive with inanimate object. The date on the door danced over Mr. Grewgius's, the knocker grinned at Mr. Scrooge, the Roman on the ceiling pointed down at Mr. Tulkinghorn, the elderly armchair leered at Tom Smart—these are all moor eeffocish things. A man sees them because he does not look at them.

And so the little Dickens Dickensized London. He prepared the way for all his personages. Into whatever cranny of our city his characters might crawl, Dickens had been there before them. However wild were the events he narrated as outside him, they could not be wilder than the things that had gone on within. However queer a character of Dickens might be, he could hardly be queerer than Dickens was. The whole secret of his after-writings is sealed up in those silent years of which no written word remains. Those years did him harm perhaps, as his biographer, Forster, has thoughtfully suggested, by sharpening a certain fierce individualism in him which once or twice during his genial life flashed like a half-hidden knife. He was always generous; but things had gone too hardly with him for him to be always easy-going. He was always kind-hearted; he was not always good-humoured. Those years may also, in their strange mixture of morbidity and reality, have increased in him his tendency to exaggeration. But we can scarcely lament this in a literary sense; exaggeration is almost the definition of art—and it is entirely the definition of Dickens' art. Those years may have given him many moral and mental wounds, from which he never recovered. But they gave him the key of the street.

There is a weird contradiction in the soul of the born optimist. He can be happy and unhappy at the same time. With Dickens the practical depression of his life at this time did nothing to prevent him from laying up those hilarious memories of which all his books are made. No doubt he was genuinely unhappy in the poor place where his mother kept school. Nevertheless it was there that he noticed the unfathomable quaintness of the little servant whom he made into the Marchioness. No doubt he was comfortless enough at the boarding-house of Mrs. Roylance; but he perceived with a dreadful joy that Mrs. Roylance's name was Pipchin. There seems to be no incompatibility between taking in tragedy and giving out comedy; they are able to run parallel in the same personality. One incident which he described

in his unfinished "autobiography," and which he
afterwards transferred almost verbatim to David
Copperfield, was peculiarly rich and impressive.
It was the inauguration of a petition to the King
for a bounty, drawn up by a committee of the
prisoners in the Marshalsea, a committee of which
Dickens's father was the president, no doubt in
virtue of his oratory, and also the scribe no doubt
in virtue of his genuine love of literary flights.

"As many of the principal officers of this body
as could be got into a small room without filling
it up, supported him in front of the petition; and
my old friend, Captain Porter (who had washed
himself to do honour to so solemn an occasion),
stationed himself close to it, to read it to all who
were unacquainted with its contents. The door
was then thrown open, and they began to come in
in a long file; several waiting on the landing outside, while one entered, affixed his signature, and
went out. To everybody in succession Captain
Porter said, 'Would you like to hear it read?'
If he weakly showed the least disposition to hear
it, Captain Porter in a loud sonorous voice gave
him every word of it. I remember a certain
luscious roll he gave to such words as "Majesty—
Gracious Majesty—Your Gracious Majesty's unfortunate subjects — Your Majesty's well-known

munificence,' as if the words were something real
in his mouth and delicious to taste : my poor
father meanwhile listening with a little of an
author's vanity and contemplating (not severely)
the spike on the opposite wall. Whatever was
comical or pathetic in this scene, I sincerely believe
I perceived in my corner, whether I demonstrated
it or not, quite as well as I should perceive it now.
I made out my own little character and story for
every man who put his name to the sheet of paper."

Here we see very plainly that Dickens did not
merely look back in after days and see that these
humours had been delightful. He was delighted
at the same moment that he was desperate. The
two opposite things existed in him simultaneously,
and each in its full strength. His soul was not a
mixed colour like grey and purple, caused by no
component colour being quite itself. His soul was
like a shot silk of black and crimson, a shot silk of
misery and joy.

Seen from the outside, his little pleasures and
extravagances seem more pathetic than his grief.
Once the solemn little figure went into a public-
house in Parliament Street, and addressed the man
behind the bar in the following terms—"What is
your very best—the VERY *best* ale a glass ?" The
man replied, "Twopence." "Then," said the infant,

"just draw me a glass of that, if you please, with a good head to it." "The landlord," says Dickens, in telling the story, "looked at me in return over the bar from head to foot with a strange smile on his face; and instead of drawing the beer looked round the screen and said something to his wife, who came out from behind it with her work in her hand and joined him in surveying me. . . . They asked me a good many questions as to what my name was, how old I was, where I lived, how I was employed, etc., etc. To all of which, that I might commit nobody, 'I invented appropriate answers. They served me with the ale, though I suspect it was not the strongest on the premises; and the landlord's wife, opening the little half-door, and bending down, gave me a kiss." Here he touches that other side of common life which he was chiefly to champion; he was to show that there is no ale like the ale of a poor man's festival, and no pleasures like the pleasures of the poor. At other places of refreshment he was yet more majestic. "I remember," he says, "tucking my own bread (which I had brought from home in the morning) under my arm, wrapt up in a piece of paper like a book, and going into the best dining-room in Johnson's Alamode Beef House in Clare Court, Drury Lane, and magnificently ordering a

small plate of *à-la-mode* beef to eat with it. What
the waiter thought of such a strange little appari-
tion coming in all alone I don't know; but I can
see him now staring at me as I ate my dinner, and
bringing up the other waiter to look. I gave him
a halfpenny, and I wish, now, that he hadn't
taken it."

For the boy individually the prospect seemed
to be growing drearier and drearier. This phrase
indeed hardly expresses the fact; for, as he felt it,
it was not so much a run of worsening luck as the
closing in of a certain and quiet calamity like the
coming on of twilight and dark. He felt that he
would die and be buried in blacking. Through all
this he does not seem to have said much to his
parents of his distress. They who were in prison
had certainly a much jollier time than he who was
free. But of all the strange ways in which the
human being proves that he is not a rational being,
whatever else he is, no case is so mysterious and
unaccountable as the secrecy of childhood. We
learn of the cruelty of some school or child-factory
from journalists; we learn it from inspectors, we
learn it from doctors, we learn it even from shame-
stricken schoolmasters and repentant sweaters;
but we never learn it from the children; we never
learn it from the victims. It would seem as if a

living creature had to be taught, like an art of culture, the art of crying out when it is hurt. It would seem as if patience were the natural thing; it would seem as if impatience were an accomplishment like whist. However this may be, it is wholly certain that Dickens might have drudged and died drudging, and buried the unborn Pickwick, but for an external accident.

He was, as has been said, in the habit of visiting his father at the Marshalsea every week. The talks between the two must have been a comedy at once more cruel and more delicate than Dickens ever described. Meredith might picture the comparison between the child whose troubles were so childish, but who felt them like a damned spirit, and the middle-aged man whose trouble was final ruin, and who felt it no more than a baby. Once, it would appear, the boy broke down altogether—perhaps under the unbearable buoyancy of his oratorical papa—and implored to be freed from the factory—implored it, I fear, with a precocious and almost horrible eloquence. The old optimist was astounded—too much astounded to do anything in particular. Whether the incident had really anything to do with what followed cannot be decided, but ostensibly it had not. Ostensibly the cause of Charles's ultimate liberation was a quarrel between

his father and Lamert, the head of the factory.
Dickens the elder (who had at last left the Marshalsea) could no doubt conduct a quarrel with the
magnificence of Micawber; the result of this talent,
at any rate, was to leave Mr. Lamert in a towering
rage. He had a stormy interview with Charles, in
which he tried to be good-tempered to the boy, but
could hardly master his tongue about the boy's
father. Finally he told him he must go, and with
every observance the little creature was solemnly
expelled from hell.

His mother, with a touch of strange harshness,
was for patching up the quarrel and sending him
back. Perhaps, with the fierce feminine responsibility, she felt that the first necessity was to keep
the family out of debt. But old John Dickens put
his foot down here—put his foot down with that
ringing but very rare decision with which (once in
ten years, and often on some trivial matter) the
weakest man will overwhelm the strongest woman.
The boy was miserable; the boy was clever; the
boy should go to school. The boy went to school;
he went to the Wellington House Academy,
Mornington Place. It was an odd experience for
any one to go from the world to a school, instead
of going from school to the world. Dickens, we
may say, had his boyhood after his youth. He had

seen life at its coarsest before he began his training
for it, and knew the worst words in the English
language probably before the best. This odd
chronology, it will be remembered, he retained in
his semi-autobiographical account of the adventures
of David Copperfield, who went into the business
of Murdstone and Grinby's before he went to the
school kept by Dr. Strong. David Copperfield,
also, went to be carefully prepared for a world that
he had seen already. Outside David Copperfield,
the records of Dickens at this time reduce themselves to a few glimpses provided by accidental
companions of his schooldays, and little can be
deduced from them about his personality beyond
a general impression of sharpness and, perhaps, of
bravado, of bright eyes and bright speeches. Probably the young creature was recuperating himself
for his misfortunes, was making the most of his
liberty, was flapping the wings of that wild spirit
that had just not been broken. We hear of things
that sound suddenly juvenile after his maturer
troubles, of a secret language sounding like mere
gibberish, and of a small theatre, with paint and
red fire, such as that which Stevenson loved. It
was not an accident that Dickens and Stevenson
loved it. It is a stage unsuited for psychological
realism ; the cardboard characters cannot analyze

each other with any effect. But it is a stage almost divinely suited for making surroundings, for making that situation and background which belongs peculiarly to romance. A toy theatre, in fact, is the opposite of private theatricals. In the latter you can do anything with the people if you do not ask much from the scenery; in the former you can do anything in scenery if you do not ask much from the people. In a toy theatre you could hardly manage a modern dialogue on marriage, but the Day of Judgment would be quite easy.

After leaving school, Dickens found employment as a clerk to Mr. Blackmore, a solicitor, as one of those inconspicuous under-clerks whom he afterwards turned to many grotesque uses. Here, no doubt, he met Lowten and Swiveller, Chuckster and Wobbler, in so far as such sacred creatures ever had embodiments on this lower earth. But it is typical of him that he had no fancy at all to remain a solicitor's clerk. The resolution to rise which had glowed in him even as a dawdling boy, when he gazed at Gads-hill, which had been darkened but not quite destroyed by his fall into the factory routine, which had been released again by his return to normal boyhood and the boundaries of school, was not likely to content itself now with the copying out of agreements. He set to work, without any advice or help, to learn to be a reporter. He worked all day at law, and then all night at shorthand. It is an art which can only be effected by time, and he had to effect it by overtime. But learning the thing under every disadvantage, without a teacher, without the possibility of concentration or complete mental force, without ordinary human sleep, he made himself one of the most rapid reporters then alive. There is a curious contrast between the casualness of the mental training to which his parents and others subjected him and the savage seriousness of the training to which he subjected himself. Somebody once asked old John Dickens where his son Charles was educated. " Well, really," said the great creature, in his spacious way, "he may be said—ah—to have educated himself." He might indeed.

This practical intensity of Dickens is worth our dwelling on, because it illustrates an elementary antithesis in his character, or what appears as an antithesis in our modern popular psychology. We are always talking about strong men against weak men; but Dickens was not only both a weak man and a strong man, he was a very weak man and also a very strong man. He was everything that we currently call a weak man; he was a man hung on wires; he was a man who might at any moment cry like a child; he was so sensitive to criticism that one may say that he lacked a skin; he was so nervous that he allowed great tragedies in his life to arise only out of nerves. But in the matter where all ordinary strong men are miserably weak — in the matter of concentrated toil and clear purpose and unconquerable worldly courage—he was like a straight sword. Mrs. Carlyle, who in her human epithets often hit the right nail so that it rang, said of him once, "He has a face made of steel." This was probably felt in a flash when she saw, in some social crowd, the clear, eager face of Dickens cutting through those near him like a knife. Any people who had met him from year to year would each year have found a man weakly troubled about his worldly decline; and each year they would have found him higher up in the world. His was a character very hard for any man of slow and placable temperament to understand; he was the character whom anybody can hurt and nobody can kill.

When he began to report in the House of Commons he was still only nineteen. His father, who had been released from his prison a short time before Charles had been released from his, had also become, among many other things, a reporter. But old John Dickens could enjoy doing anything without any particular aspiration after doing it well. But Charles was of a very different temper. He was, as I have said, consumed with an enduring and almost angry thirst to excel. He learnt shorthand with a dark self-devotion as if it were a sacred hieroglyph. Of this self-instruction, as of everything else, he has left humorous and illuminating phrases. He describes how, after he had learnt the whole exact alphabet, "there then appeared a procession of new horrors, called arbitrary characters—the most despotic characters I have ever known ; who insisted, for instance, that a thing like the beginning of a cobweb meant ' expectation,' and that a pen-and-ink skyrocket stood for 'disadvantageous.'" He concludes, "It was almost heartbreaking." But it is significant that somebody else, a colleague of his, concluded, "There never *was* such a shorthand writer."

Dickens succeeded in becoming a shorthand writer; succeeded in becoming a reporter; succeeded ultimately in becoming a highly effective journalist. He was appointed as a reporter of the speeches in Parliament, first by *The True Sun*, then by *The Mirror of Parliament*, and last by *The Morning Chronicle*. He reported the speeches very well, and if we must analyze his internal opinions, much better than they deserved. For it must be remembered that this lad went into the reporter's gallery full of the triumphant Radicalism which was then the rising tide of the world. He was, it must be confessed, very little overpowered by the dignity of the Mother of Parliaments : he regarded the House of Commons much as he regarded the House of Lords, as a sort of venerable joke. It was, perhaps, while he watched, pale with weariness from the reporter's gallery, that there sank into him a thing that never left him, his unfathomable contempt for the British Constitution. Then perhaps he heard from the Government benches the immortal apologies of the Circumlocution Office. " Then would the noble lord or right honourable gentleman, in whose department it was to defend the Circumlocution Office, put an orange in his pocket, and make a regular field-day of the occasion. Then would he come down to that house with a slap upon the table and meet the honourable gentleman foot to foot. Then would he be there to tell that honourable gentleman that the Circumlocution Office was not only blameless in this matter, but was commendable in this matter, was extollable to the skies in this matter. Then would he be there to tell that honourable gentleman that although the Circumlocution Office was invariably right, and wholly right, it never was so right as in this matter. Then would he be there to tell the honourable gentleman that it would have been more to his honour, more to his credit, more to his good taste, more to his good sense, more to half the dictionary of common places if he had left the Circumlocution Office alone and never approached this matter. Then would he keep one eye upon a coach or crammer from the Circumlocution Office below the bar, and smash the honourable gentleman with the Circumlocution Office account of this matter. And although one of two things always happened ; namely, either that the Circumlocution Office had nothing to say, and said it, or that it had something to say of which the noble lord or right honourable gentleman blundered one half and forgot the other ; the Circumlocution Office was always voted immaculate by an accommo-dating majority." We are now generally told that Dickens has destroyed these abuses, and that this is no longer a true picture of public life. Such, at any rate, is the Circumlocution Office account of this matter. But Dickens as a good Radical would, I fancy, much prefer that we should continue his battle than that we should celebrate his triumph ; es-pecially when it has not come. England is still ruled by the great Barnacle family. Parliament is still ruled by the great Barnacle trinity—the solemn old

Barnacle, who knew that the Circumlocution Office was a protection, the sprightly young Barnacle who knew that it was a fraud, and the bewildered young Barnacle who knew nothing about it. From these three types our Cabinets are still exclusively recruited. People talk of the tyrannies and anomalies which Dickens denounced as things of the past like the Star Chamber. They believe that the days of the old stupid optimism and the old brutal indifference are gone for ever. In truth, this very belief is only the continuance of the old stupid optimism and the old brutal indifference. We believe in a free England and a pure England, because we still believe in the Circumlocution Office account of this matter. Undoubtedly our serenity is wide-spread. We believe that England is really reformed, we believe that England is really democratic, we believe that English politics are free from corruption. But this general satisfaction of ours does not show that Dickens has beaten the Barnacles. It only shows that the Barnacles have beaten Dickens.

It cannot be too often said, then, that we must read into young Dickens and his works this old Radical tone towards institutions. That tone was a sort of happy impatience. And when Dickens had to listen for hours to the speech of the noble

lord in defence of the Circumlocution Office, when,
that is, he had to listen to what he regarded as the
last vaporings of a vanishing oligarchy, the impatience rather predominated over the happiness.
His incurably restless nature found more pleasure
in the wandering side of journalism. He went
about wildly in post-chaises to report political
meetings for the *Morning Chronicle.* "And what
gentlemen they were to serve," he exclaimed, "in
such things at the old *Morning Chronicle.* Great
or small it did not matter. I have had to charge for
half a dozen breakdowns in half a dozen times as
many miles. I have had to charge for the damage
of a great-coat from the drippings of a blazing wax
candle, in writing through the smallest hours of the
night in a swift flying carriage and pair." And again,
"I have often transcribed for the printer from my
shorthand notes important public speeches in which
the strictest accuracy was required, and a mistake
in which would have been to a young man severely
compromising, writing on the palm of my hand, by
the light of a dark lantern, in a post-chaise and
four, galloping through a wild country and through
the dead of the night, at the then surprising rate of
fifteen miles an hour." The whole of Dickens's
life goes with the throb of that nocturnal gallop.
All its real wildness shot through with an

imaginative wickedness he afterwards uttered in
the drive of Jonas Chuzzlewit through the storm.

All this time, and indeed from a time of which
no measure can be taken, the creative part of his
mind had been in a stir or even a fever. While
still a small boy he had written for his own amusement some sketches of queer people he had met;
notably, one of his uncle's barber, whose principal
hobby was pointing out what Napoleon ought to
have done in the matter of military tactics. He
had a note-book full of such sketches. He had
sketches not only of persons, but of places, which
were to him almost more personal than persons.
In the December of 1833 he published one of these
fragments in the *Old Monthly Magazine*. This was
followed by nine others in the same paper, and
when the paper (which was a romantically Radical
venture, run by a veteran soldier of Bolivar) itself
collapsed, Dickens continued the series in the
Evening Chronicle, an off-shoot of the morning
paper of the same name. These were the pieces
afterwards published and known as the "Sketches
by Boz"; and with them Dickens enters literature.
He also enters upon many things about this time;
he enters manhood, and among other things
marriage. A friend of his on the *Chronicle*, George
Hogarth, had several daughters. With all of them

Dickens appears to have been on terms of great affection. This sketch is wholly literary, and I do not feel it necessary to do more than touch upon such incidents as his marriage, just as I shall do no more than touch upon the tragedy that ultimately overtook it. But it may be suggested here that the final misfortunes were in some degree due to the circumstances attending the original action. A very young man fighting his way, and excessively poor, with no memories for years past that were not monotonous and mean, and with his strongest and most personal memories quite ignominious and unendurable, was suddenly thrown into the society of a whole family of girls. I think it 'does not overstate his weakness, and I think it partly constitutes his excuse, to say that he fell in love with all of them. As sometimes happens in the undeveloped youth, an abstract femininity simply intoxicated him. And again, I think we shall not be mistakenly accused of harshness if we put the point in this way; that by a kind of accident he got hold of the wrong sister. In what came afterwards he was enormously to blame. But I do not think that his was a case of cold division from a woman whom he had once seriously and singly loved. He had been bewildered in a burning haze, I will not say even of first love, but of first flirtations.

His wife's sisters stimulated him before he fell in love with his wife; and they continued to stimulate him long after he had quarrelled with her for ever. This view is strikingly supported by all the details of his attitude towards all the other members of the sacred house of Hogarth. One of the sisters remained, of course, his dearest friend till death. Another who had died, he worshipped as a saint, and he always asked to be buried in her grave. He was married on April 2, 1836. Forster remarks that a few days before the announcement of their marriage in the *Times*, the same paper contained another announcement that on the 31st would be published the first number of a work called "The Posthumous Papers of the Pickwick Club." It is the beginning of his career.

The "Sketches," apart from splendid splashes of humour here and there, are not manifestations of the man of genius. We might almost say that this book is one of the few books by Dickens which would not, standing alone, have made his fame. And yet standing alone it did make his fame. His contemporaries could see a new spirit in it, where we, familiar with the larger fruits of that spirit, can only see a continuation of the prosaic and almost wooden wit of the comic books of that day. But in any case we should hardly look in the man's first

book for the fulness of his contribution to letters.
Youth is almost everything else, but it is hardly
ever original. We read of young men bursting on
the old world with a new message. But youth in
actual experience is the period of imitation and
even of obedience. Subjectively its emotions may
be furious and headlong; but its only external
outcome is a furious imitation and a headlong
obedience. As we grow older we learn the special
thing we have to do. As a man goes on towards
the grave he discovers gradually a philosophy he
can really call fresh, a style he can really call his
own, and as he becomes an older man he becomes
a newer writer. Ibsen, in his youth, wrote almost
classic plays about vikings; it was in his old age
that he began to break windows and throw fire-
works. The only fault, it was said, of Browning's
first poems was that they had "too much beauty of
imagery, and too little wealth of thought." The
only fault, that is, of Browning's first poems, was
that they were not Browning's.

In one way, however, the "Sketches by Boz" do
stand out very symbolically in the life of Dickens.
They constitute in a manner the dedication of
him to his especial task; the sympathetic and
yet exaggerated painting of the poorer middle-
class. He was to make men feel that this dull

middle-class was actually a kind of elf-land. But here, again, the work is rude and undeveloped; and this is shown in the fact that it is a great deal more exaggerative than it is sympathetic. We are not, of course, concerned with the kind of people who say that they wish that Dickens was more refined. If those people are ever refined it will be by fire. But there is in this earliest work, an element which almost vanished in the later ones, an element which is typical of the middle-classes in England, and which is in a more real sense to be called vulgar. I mean that in these little farces there is a trace, in the author as well as in the characters, of that petty sense of social precedence, that hub-bub of little unheard-of oligarchies, which is the only serious sin of the bourgeoisie of Britain. It may seem pragmatical, for example, to instance such a rowdy farce as the story of Horatio Sparkins, which tells how a tuft-hunting family entertained a rhetorical youth thinking he was a lord, and found he was a draper's assistant. No doubt they were very snobbish in thinking that a lord must be eloquent; but we cannot help feeling that Dickens is almost equally snobbish in feeling it so very funny that a draper's assistant should be eloquent. A free man, one would think, would despise the family quite as

much if Horatio had been a peer.   Here, and here
only, there is just a touch of the vulgarity, of the
only vulgarity of the world out of which Dickens
came.   For the only element of lowness that there
really is in our populace is exactly that they are
full of superiorities and very conscious of class.
Shades, imperceptible to the eyes of others, but
as hard and haughty as a Brahmin caste, separate
one kind of charwoman from another kind of
charwoman.   Dickens was destined to show with
inspired symbolism all the immense virtues of the
democracy.   He was to show them as the most
humorous part of our civilization; which they
certainly are.   He was to show them as the most
promptly and practically compassionate part of
our civilization; which they certainly are.   The
democracy has a hundred exuberant good qualities;
the democracy has only one outstanding sin—it is
not democratic.

CHAPTER IV

"THE PICKWICK PAPERS"

ROUND the birth of "Pickwick" broke one
of those literary quarrels that were too
common in the life of Dickens. Such quarrels
indeed generally arose from some definite mistake
or misdemeanour on the part of somebody else;
but they were also made possible by an indefinite
touchiness and susceptibility in Dickens himself.
He was so sensitive on points of personal authorship and responsibility that even his sacred sense
of humour deserted him. He turned people into
mortal enemies whom he might have turned very
easily into immortal jokes. It was not that he
was lawless: in a sense it was that he was too
legal; but he did not understand the principle of
de minimis non curat lex. Anybody could draw
him; any fool could make a fool of him. Any
obscure madman who chose to say that he had
written the whole of "Martin Chuzzlewit;" any
penny-a-liner who chose to say that Dickens wore
no shirt-collar, could call forth the most passionate
and public denials as of a man pleading "not

guilty" to witchcraft or high treason. Hence the
letters of Dickens are filled with a certain singular
type of quarrels and complaints, quarrels and complaints in which one cannot say that he was on the
wrong side, but merely that even in being on the
right side he was in the wrong place. He was not
only a generous man, he was even a just man; to have
made against anybody a charge or claim which was
unfair would have been insupportable to him. His
weakness was that he found the unfair claim or
charge, however small, equally insupportable when
brought against himself. No one can say of him that
he was often wrong; we can only say of him as of
many pugnacious people, that he was too often right.

The incidents attending the inauguration of the
"Pickwick Papers" are not, perhaps, a perfect
example of this trait, because Dickens was here
a hand-to-mouth journalist, and the blow might
possibly have been more disabling than those
struck at him in his days of triumph. But all
through those days of triumph, and to the day of
his death, Dickens took this old tea-cup tempest
with the most terrible gravity, drew up declarations, called witnesses, preserved pulverizing documents, and handed on to his children the forgotten
folly as if it had been a Highland feud. Yet the
unjust claim made on him was so much more

ridiculous even than it was unjust, that it seems strange that he should have remembered it for a month except for his amusement. The facts are simple and familiar to most people. The publishers —Chapman & Hall—wished to produce some kind of serial with comic illustrations by a popular caricaturist named Seymour. This artist was chiefly famous for his rendering of the farcical side of sport, and to suit this speciality it was very vaguely suggested to Dickens by the publishers that he should write about a Nimrod Club, or some such thing, a club of amateur sportsmen, foredoomed to perpetual ignominies. Dickens objected in substance upon two very sensible grounds—first, that sporting sketches were stale; and second, that he knew nothing about sport. He changed the idea to that of a general club for travel and investigation, the Pickwick Club, and only retained one fated sportsman, Mr. Winkle, the melancholy remnant of the Nimrod Club that never was. The first seven pictures appeared with the signature of Seymour and the letterpress of Dickens, and in them Winkle and his woes were fairly, but not extraordinarily prominent. Before the eighth picture appeared Seymour had blown his brains out. After a brief interval of the employment of a man named Buss, Dickens obtained the assistance of

Hablot K. Browne, whom we all call "Phiz," and may almost, in a certain sense, be said to have gone into partnership with him. They were as suited to each other and to the common creation of a unique thing as Gilbert and Sullivan. No other illustrator ever created the true Dickens characters with the precise and correct quantum of exaggeration. No other illustrator ever breathed the true Dickens atmosphere, in which clerks are clerks and yet at the same time elves.

To the tame mind the above affair does not seem to offer anything very promising in the way of a row. But Seymour's widow managed to evolve out of it the proposition that somehow or other her husband had written "Pickwick," or, at least, had been responsible for the genius and success of it. It does not appear that she had anything at all resembling a reason for this opinion except the unquestionable fact that the publishers had started with the idea of employing Seymour. This was quite true, and Dickens (who over and above his honesty was far too quarrelsome a man not to try to keep in the right, and who showed a sort of fierce carefulness in telling the truth in such cases) never denied it or attempted to conceal it. It was quite true, that at the beginning, instead of Seymour being employed to illustrate Dickens,

Dickens may be said to have been employed to illustrate Seymour. But that Seymour invented anything in the letter-press large or small, that he invented either the outline of Mr. Pickwick's character or the number of Mr. Pickwick's cabman, that he invented either the story, or so much as a semi-colon in the story was not only never proved, but was never very lucidly alleged. Dickens fills his letters with all that there is to be said against Mrs. Seymour's idea; it is not very clear whether there was ever anything definitely said for it.

Upon the mere superficial fact and law of the affair, Dickens ought to have been superior to this silly business. But in a much deeper and a much more real sense he ought to have been superior to it. It did not really touch him or his greatness at all, even as an abstract allegation. If Seymour had started the story, had provided Dickens with his puppets, Tupmen or Jingle, Dickens would have still have been Dickens and Seymour only Seymour. As a matter of fact, it happened to be a contemptible lie, but it would have been an equally contemptible truth. For the fact is that the greatness of Dickens and especially the greatness of Pickwick is not of a kind that could be affected by somebody else suggesting the first idea. It could not be affected by somebody else writing the first

chapter. If it could be shown that another man
had suggested to Hawthorne (let us say) the
primary conception of the "Scarlet Letter," Hawthorne who worked it out would still be an
exquisite workman; but he would be by so much
less a creator. But in a case like Pickwick there
is a simple test. If Seymour gave Dickens the
main idea of Pickwick, what was it? There is
no primary conception of Pickwick for any one to
suggest. Dickens not only did not get the general
plan from Seymour, he did not get it at all. In
Pickwick, and, indeed, in Dickens, generally it
is in the details that the author is creative, it is in
the details that he is vast. The power of the book
lies in the perpetual torrent of ingenious and
inventive treatment; the theme (at least at the
beginning) simply does not exist. The idea of
Tupman, the fat lady-killer, is in itself quite dreary
and vulgar; it is the detailed Tupman, as he is developed, who is unexpectedly amusing. The idea
of Winkle, the clumsy sportsman, is in itself quite
stale; it is, as he goes on repeating himself, that he
becomes original. We hear of men whose imagination can touch with magic the dull facts of our
life, but Dickens's yet more indomitable fancy
could touch with magic even our dull fiction.
Before we are halfway through the book the stock

characters of dead and damned farces astonish us like splendid strangers.

Seymour's claim, then, viewed symbolically, was even a compliment. It was true in spirit that Dickens obtained (or might have obtained) the start of Pickwick from somebody else, from anybody else. For he had a more gigantic energy than the energy of the intense artist, the energy which is prepared to write something. He had the energy which is prepared to write anything. He could have finished any man's tale. He could have breathed a mad life into any man's characters. If it had been true that Seymour had planned out Pickwick, if Seymour had fixed the chapters and named and numbered the characters, his slave would have shown even in these shackles such a freedom as would have shaken the world. If Dickens had been forced to make his incidents out of a chapter in a child's reading-book, or the names in a scrap of newspaper, he would have turned them in ten pages into creatures of his own. Seymour, as I say, was in a manner right in spirit. Dickens would at this time get his materials from anywhere, in the sense that he cared little what materials they were. He would not have stolen; but if he had stolen he would never have imitated. The power which he proceeded at once to exhibit was the one power in letters which literally cannot be imitated, the primary inexhaustible creative energy, the enormous prodigality of genius which no one but another genius could parody. To claim to have originated an idea of Dickens is like claiming to have contributed a glass of water to Niagara. Wherever this stream or that stream started the colossal cataract of absurdity went roaring night and day. The volume of his invention overwhelmed all doubt of his inventiveness; Dickens was evidently a great man; unless he was a thousand men.

The actual circumstances of the writing and publishing of "Pickwick" show that while Seymour's specific claim was absurd, Dickens's indignant exactitude about every jot and tittle of authorship was also inappropriate and misleading. "The Pickwick Papers," when all is said and done, did emerge out of a haze of suggestions and proposals in which more than one person was involved. The publishers failed to base the story on a Nimrod Club, but they succeeded in basing it on a club. Seymour, by virtue of his idiosyncrasy, if he did not create, brought about the creation of Mr. Winkle. Seymour sketched Mr. Pickwick as a tall, thin man. Mr. Chapman (apparently without any word from Dickens) boldly turned him into a

short, fat man. Chapman took the type from a
corpulent old dandy named Foster, who wore tights
and gaiters and lived at Richmond. In this sense,
were we affected by this idle aspect of the thing,
we might call Chapman the real originator of
"Pickwick." But as I have suggested, originating
"Pickwick" is not the point. It was quite easy to
originate " Pickwick." The difficulty was to write it.

However such things may be, there can be no
question of the result of this chaos. In "The
Pickwick Papers" Dickens sprang suddenly from a
comparatively low level to a very high one. To
the level of "Sketches by Boz" he never afterwards descended. To the level of "The Pickwick
Papers" it is doubtful if he ever afterwards rose.
"Pickwick," indeed, is not a good novel; but it is
not a bad novel, for it is not a novel at all. In one
sense, indeed, it is something nobler than a novel,
for no novel with a plot and a proper termination
could emit that sense of everlasting youth—a sense
as of the gods gone wandering in England. This
is not a novel, for all novels have an end; and
"Pickwick," properly speaking, has no end—he is
equal unto the angels. The point at which, as a
fact, we find the printed matter terminates is not
an end in any artistic sense of the word. Even as
a boy I believed there were some more pages that

were torn out of my copy, and I am looking for
them still. The book might have been cut short
anywhere else. It might have been cut short after
Mr. Pickwick was released by Mr. Nupkins, or
after Mr. Pickwick was fished out of the water, or
at a hundred other places. And we should still
have known that this was not really the story's
end. We should have known that Mr. Pickwick
was still having the same high adventures on the
same high roads. As it happens, the book ends
after Mr. Pickwick has taken a house in the neighbourhood of Dulwich. But we know he did not
stop there. We know he broke out, that he took
again the road of the high adventures; we know
that if we take it ourselves in any acre of England,
we may come suddenly upon him in a lane.

But this relation of "Pickwick" to the strict
form of fiction demands a further word, which
should indeed be said in any case before the consideration of any or all of the Dickens tales.
Dickens's work is not to be reckoned in novels at
all. Dickens's work is to be reckoned always by
characters, sometimes by groups, oftener by episodes, but never by novels. You cannot discuss
whether "Nicholas Nickleby" is a good novel, or
whether "Our Mutual Friend" is a bad novel.
Strictly, there is no such novel as "Nicholas

Nickleby." There is no such novel as "Our Mutual
Friend." They are simply lengths cut from the
flowing and mixed substance called Dickens—a
substance of which any given length will be certain
to contain a given proportion of brilliant and
of bad stuff. You can say, according to your
opinions, "the Crummles part is perfect," or "the
Boffins are a mistake," just as a man watching a
river go by him could count here a floating flower,
and there a streak of scum. But you cannot artistically divide the output into books. The best of his
work can be found in the worst of his works.
"The Tale of Two Cities" is a good novel; "Little
Dorrit" is not a good novel. But the description
of "The Circumlocution Office" in "Little Dorrit"
is quite as good as the description of "Tellson's
Bank" in "The Tale of Two Cities." "The Old
Curiosity Shop" is not so good as "David Copperfield," but Swiveller is quite as good as Micawber.
Nor is there any reason why these superb creatures, as a general rule, should be in one novel any
more than another. There is no reason why Sam
Weller, in the course of his wanderings, should not
wander into "Nicholas Nickleby." There is no
reason why Major Bagstock, in his brisk way,
should not walk straight out of "Dombey and
Son" and straight into "Martin Chuzzlewit." To

this generalization some modification should be added. "Pickwick" stands by itself, and has even a sort of unity in not pretending to unity. "David Copperfield," in a less degree, stands by itself, as being the only book in which Dickens wrote of himself; and "The Tale of Two Cities" stands by itself as being the only book in which Dickens slightly altered himself. But as a whole, this should be firmly grasped, that the units of Dickens, the primary elements, are not the stories, but the characters who affect the stories—or, more often still, the characters who do not affect the stories.

This is a plain matter; but, unless it be stated and felt, Dickens may be greatly misunderstood and greatly underrated. For not only is his whole machinery directed to facilitating the self-display of certain characters, but something more deep and more unmodern still is also true of him. It is also true that all the *moving* machinery exists only to display entirely *static* character. Things in the Dickens story shift and change only in order to give us glimpses of great characters that do not change at all. If we had a sequel of Pickwick ten years afterwards, Pickwick would be exactly the same age. We know he would not have fallen into that strange and beautiful second childhood which soothed and simplified the end of Colonel

Newcome. Newcome, throughout the book, is in an atmosphere of time : Pickwick, throughout the book, is not. This will probably be taken by most modern people as praise of Thackeray and dispraise of Dickens. But this only shows how few modern people understand Dickens. It also shows how few understand the faiths and the fables of mankind. The matter can only be roughly stated in one way. Dickens did not strictly make a literature ; he made a mythology.

For a few years our corner of Western Europe has had a fancy for this thing we call fiction ; that is, for writing down our own lives or similar lives in order to look at them. But though we call it fiction, it differs from older literatures chiefly in being less fictitious. It imitates not only life, but the limitations of life ; it not only reproduces life, it reproduces death. But outside us, in every other country, in every other age, there has been going on from the beginning a more fictitious kind of fiction. I mean the kind now called folklore, the literature of the people. Our modern novels, which deal with men as they are, are chiefly produced by a small and educated section of the society. But this other literature deals with men greater than they are—with demi-gods and heroes ; and that is far too important a matter to be trusted to the educated classes. The fashioning of these portents is a popular trade, like ploughing or bricklaying; the men who made hedges, the men who made ditches, were the men who made deities. Men could not elect their kings, but they could elect their gods. So we find ourselves faced with a fundamental contrast between what is called fiction and what is called folklore. The one exhibits an abnormal degree of dexterity operating within our daily limitations; the other exhibits quite normal desires extended beyond those limitations. Fiction means the common things as seen by the uncommon people. Fairy tales mean the uncommon things as seen by the common people.

As our world advances through history towards its present epoch, it becomes more specialist, less democratic, and folklore turns gradually into fiction. But it is only slowly that the old elfin fire fades into the light of common realism. For ages after our characters have dressed up in the clothes of mortals they betray the blood of the gods. Even our phraseology is full of relics of this. When a modern novel is devoted to the bewilderments of a weak young clerk who cannot decide which woman he wants to marry, or which new religion he believes in, we still give this knock-kneed cad the name of "the hero"—the name which is the crown of Achilles. The popular preference for a story with "a happy ending" is not, or at least was not, a mere sweet-stuff optimism; it is the remains of the old idea of the triumph of the dragon-slayer, the ultimate apotheosis of the man beloved of heaven.

But there is another and more intangible trace of this fading supernaturalism—a trace very vivid to the reader, but very elusive to the critic. It is a certain air of endlessness in the episodes, even in the shortest episodes—a sense that, although we leave them, they still go on. Our modern attraction to short stories is not an accident of form; it is the sign of a real sense of fleetingness and fragility; it means that existence is only an impression, and, perhaps, only an illusion. A short story of to-day has the air of a dream; it has the irrevocable beauty of a falsehood; we get a glimpse of grey streets of London or red plains of India, as in an opium vision; we see people—arresting people with fiery and appealing faces. But when the story is ended, the people are ended. We have no instinct of anything ultimate and enduring behind the episodes. The moderns, in a word, describe life in short stories because they are possessed with the sentiment that life itself is an uncommonly short story, and perhaps not a true one. But in this elder literature, even in the comic literature (indeed, especially in the comic literature), the reverse is true. The characters are felt to be fixed things of which we have fleeting glimpses ; that is, they are felt to be divine. Uncle Toby is talking for ever, as the elves are dancing for ever. We feel that whenever we hammer on the house of Falstaff, Falstaff will be at home. We feel it as a Pagan would feel that, if a cry broke the silence after ages of unbelief, Apollo would still be listening in his temple. These writers may tell short stories, but we feel they are only parts of a long story. And herein lies the peculiar significance, the peculiar sacredness even, of penny dreadfuls and the common printed matter made for our errand-boys. Here in dim and desperate forms, under the ban of our base culture, stormed at by silly magistrates, sneered at by silly schoolmasters, —here is the old popular literature still popular ; here is the unmistakable voluminousness, the thousand and one tales of Dick Deadshot, like the thousand and one tales of Robin Hood. Here is the splendid and static boy, the boy who remains a boy through a thousand volumes and a thousand years. Here in mean alleys and dim shops, shadowed and shamed by the police, mankind is still driving its dark trade in heroes. And elsewhere,

and in all other ages, in braver fashion, under
cleaner skies, the same eternal tale-telling goes on,
and the whole mortal world is a factory of immortals.

Dickens was a mythologist rather than a
novelist; he was the last of the mythologists, and
perhaps the greatest. He did not always manage
to make his characters men, but he always
managed, at the least, to make them gods. They
are creatures like Punch or Father Christmas.
They live statically, in a perpetual summer of
being themselves. It was not the aim of Dickens
to show the effect of time and circumstance upon
a character; it was not even his aim to show the
effect of a character on time and circumstance. It
is worth remark, in passing, that whenever he tried
to describe change in a character, he made a mess
of it, as in the repentance of Dombey or the apparent deterioration of Boffin. It was his aim to
show character hung in a kind of happy void, in a
world apart from time—yes, and essentially apart
from circumstance, though the phrase may seem
odd in connection with the godlike horse-play of
"Pickwick." But all the Pickwickian events, wild
as they often are, were only designed to display
the greater wildness of souls, or sometimes merely
to bring the reader within touch, so to speak, of
that wildness. The author would have fired Mr.

Pickwick out of a cannon to get him to Wardle's by Christmas; he would have taken the roof off to drop him into Bob Sawyer's party. But once put Pickwick at Wardle's, with his punch and a group of gorgeous personalities, and nothing will move him from his chair. Once he is at Sawyer's party, he forgets how he got there; he forgets Mrs. Bardell and all his story. For the story was but an incantation to call up a god, and the god (Mr. Jack Hopkins) is present in divine power. Once the great characters are face to face, the ladder by which they climbed is forgotten and falls down, the structure of the story drops to pieces, the plot is abandoned, the other characters deserted at every kind of crisis; the whole crowded thorough-fare of the tale is blocked by two or three talkers, who take their immortal ease as if they were already in Paradise. For they do not exist for the story; the story exists for them; and they know it.

To every man alive, one must hope, it has in some manner happened that he has talked with his more fascinating friends round a table on some night when all the numerous personalities unfolded themselves like great tropical flowers. All fell into their parts as in some delightful impromptu play. Every man was more himself than he had ever been in this vale of tears. Every man was a beautiful caricature of himself. The man who has known such nights will understand the exaggerations of "Pickwick." The man who has not known such nights will not enjoy "Pickwick" nor (I imagine) heaven. For, as I have said, Dickens is, in this matter, close to popular religion, which is the ultimate and reliable religion. He conceives an endless joy; he conceives creatures as permanent as Puck or Pan— creatures whose will to live æons upon æons cannot satisfy. He is not come, as a writer, that his creatures may copy life and copy its narrowness; he is come that they may have life, and that they may have it more abundantly. It is absurd indeed that Christians should be called the enemies of life because they wish life to last for ever; it is more absurd still to call the old comic writers dull because they wished their unchanging characters to last for ever. Both popular religion, with its endless joys, and the old comic story, with its endless jokes, have in our time faded together. We are too weak to desire that undying vigour. We believe that you can have too much of a good thing —a blasphemous belief, which at one blow wrecks all the heavens that men have hoped for. The grand old defiers of God were not afraid of an eternity of torment. We have come to be afraid of an eternity of joy. It is not my business here to take sides in this division between those who like life and long novels and those who like death and short stories; my only business is to point out that those who see in Dickens's unchanging characters and recurring catch-words a mere stiffness and lack of living movement miss the point and nature of his work. His tradition is another tradition altogether; his aim is another aim altogether to those of the modern novelists who trace the alchemy of experience and the autumn tints of character. He is there, like the common people of all ages, to make deities; he is there, as I have said, to exaggerate life in the direction of life. The spirit he at bottom celebrates is that of two friends drinking wine together and talking through the night. But for him they are two deathless friends talking through an endless night and pouring wine from an inexhaustible bottle.

This, then, is the first firm fact to grasp about " Pickwick "—about Pickwick more than about any of the other stories. It is, first and foremost, a supernatural story. Mr. Pickwick was a fairy. So was old Mr. Weller. This does not imply that they were suited to swing in a trapeze of gossamer; it merely implies that if they had fallen out of it on their heads they would not have died. But, to speak more strictly, Mr. Samuel Pickwick is not the fairy ; he is the fairy prince ; that is to say, he is the abstract wanderer and wonderer, the Ulysses of comedy ; the half-human and half-elfin creature —human enough to wander, human enough to wonder, but still sustained with that merry fatalism that is natural to immortal beings—sustained by that hint of divinity which tells him in the darkest hour that he is doomed to live happily ever afterwards. He has set out walking to the end of the world, but he knows he will find an inn there.

And this brings us to the best and boldest element of originality in " Pickwick." It has not, I think, been observed, and it may be that Dickens did not observe it. Certainly he did not plan it ; it grew gradually, perhaps out of the unconscious part of his soul, and warmed the whole story like a slow fire. Of course it transformed the whole story also ; transformed it out of all likeness to itself. About this latter point was waged one of the numberless little wars of Dickens. It was a part of his pugnacious vanity that he refused to admit the truth of the mildest criticism. Moreover, he used his inexhaustible ingenuity to find an apologia that was generally an afterthought. Instead of laughingly admitting, in answer to criticism, the glorious improbability of Pecksniff, he retorted with a sneer, clever and very unjust, that he was not surprised that the Pecksniffs should deny the portrait of Pecksniff. When it was objected that the pride of old Paul Dombey breaks as abruptly as a stick, he tried to make out that there had been an absorbing psychological struggle going on in that gentleman all the time, which the reader was too stupid to perceive. Which is, I am afraid, rubbish. And so, in a similar vein, he answered those who pointed out to him the obvious and not very shocking fact that our sentiments about Pickwick are very different in the second part of the book from our sentiments in the first; that we find ourselves at the beginning setting out in the company of a farcical old fool, if not a farcical old humbug, and that we find ourselves at the end saying farewell to a fine old English merchant, a monument of genial sanity. Dickens answered with the same ingenious self-justification as in the other cases—that surely it often happened that a man met us first arrayed in his more grotesque qualities, and that fuller acquaintance unfolded his more serious merits. This, of course, is quite true; but I think any honest admirer of "Pickwick" will feel that it is not an answer. For the fault in "Pickwick" (if it be a fault) is a change not in the hero but in the whole atmosphere. The point is not that Pickwick turns into a different

kind of man; it is that "The Pickwick Papers"
turns into a different kind of book. And however
artistic both parts may be, this combination must,
in strict art, be called inartistic. A man is quite
artistically justified in writing a tale in which a
man as cowardly as Bob Acres becomes a man as
brave as Hector. But a man is not artistically
justified in writing a tale which begins in the style
of "The Rivals" and ends in the style of the
"Iliad." In other words, we do not mind the hero
changing in the course of a book; but we are not
prepared for the author changing in the course of
the book. And the author did change in the course
of this book. He made, in the midst of this book
a great discovery, which was the discovery of his
destiny, or, what is more important, of his duty.
That discovery turned him from the author of
"Sketches by Boz" to the author of "David
Copperfield." And that discovery constituted the
thing of which I have spoken—the outstanding and
arresting original feature in " The Pickwick Papers."

"Pickwick," I have said, is a romance of
adventure, and Samuel Pickwick is the romantic
adventurer. So much is indeed obvious. But the
strange and stirring discovery which Dickens made
was this—that having chosen a fat old man of the
middle classes as a good thing of which to make

a butt, he found that a fat old man of the middle classes is the very best thing of which to make a romantic adventurer. "Pickwick" is supremely original in that it is the adventures of an old man. It is a fairy tale in which the victor is not the youngest of the three brothers, but one of the oldest of their uncles. The result is both noble and new and true. There is nothing which so much needs simplicity as adventure. And there is no one who so much possesses simplicity as an honest and elderly man of business. For romance he is better than a troop of young troubadours; for the swaggering young fellow anticipates his adventures, just as he anticipates his income. Hence both the adventures and the income, when he comes up to them, are not there. But a man in late middle-age has grown used to the plain necessities, and his first holiday is a second youth. A good man, as Thackeray said with such thorough and searching truth, grows simpler as he grows older. Samuel Pickwick in his youth was probably an insufferable young coxcomb. He knew then, or thought he knew, all about the confidence tricks of swindlers like Jingle. He knew then, or thought he knew, all about the amatory designs of sly ladies like Mrs. Bardell. But years and real life have relieved him of this idle and evil knowledge.

He has had the high good luck in losing the follies
of youth to lose the wisdom of youth also.
Dickens has caught, in a manner at once wild and
convincing, this queer innocence of the afternoon
of life. The round, moon-like face, the round,
moon-like spectacles of Samuel Pickwick move
through the tale as emblems of a certain spherical
simplicity. They are fixed in that grave surprise
that may be seen in babies; that grave surprise
which is the only real happiness that is possible
to man. Pickwick's round face is like a round and
honourable mirror, in which are reflected all the
fantasies of earthly existence; for surprise is,
strictly speaking, the only kind of reflection. All
this grew gradually on Dickens. It is odd to recall
to our minds the original plan, the plan of the
Nimrod Club, and the author who was to be
wholly occupied in playing practical jokes on his
characters. He had chosen (or somebody else had
chosen) that corpulent old simpleton as a person
peculiarly fitted to fall down trap-doors, to shoot
over butter slides, to struggle with apple-pie beds,
to be tipped out of carts and dipped into horse-
ponds. But Dickens, and Dickens only, discovered
as he went on how fitted the fat old man was to
rescue ladies, to defy tyrants, to dance, to leap,
to experiment with life, to be a *deus ex machinâ*,

and even a knight errant. Dickens made this discovery. Dickens went into the Pickwick Club to scoff, and Dickens remained to pray.

Molière and his marquises are very much amused when M. Jourdain, the fat old middle-class fellow, discovers with delight that he has been talking prose all his life. I have often wondered whether Moliere saw how in this fact M. Jourdain towers above them all and touches the stars. He has the freshness to enjoy a fresh fact, the freshness to enjoy even an old one. He can feel that the common thing prose is an accomplishment like verse; and it is an accomplishment like verse; it is the miracle of language. He can feel the subtle taste of water, and roll it on his tongue like wine. His simple vanity and voracity, his innocent love of living, his ignorant love of learning, are things far fuller of romance than the weariness and foppishness of the sniggering cavaliers. When he consciously speaks prose, he unconsciously thinks poetry. It would be better for us all if we were as conscious that supper is supper or that life is life, as this true romantic was that prose is actually prose. M. Jourdain is here the type, Mr. Pickwick is elsewhere the type, of this true and neglected thing, the romance of the middle classes. It is the custom in our little epoch to sneer at the middle classes. Cockney artists profess to find the bourgeoisie dull; as if artists had any business to find anything dull. Decadents talk contemptuously of its conventions and its set tasks; it never occurs to them that conventions and set tasks are the very way to keep that greenness in the grass and that redness in the roses—which they have lost for ever. Stevenson, in his incomparable "Lantern Bearers," describes the ecstasy of a schoolboy in the mere fact of buttoning a dark lantern under a dark great-coat. If you wish for that ecstasy of the schoolboy, you must have the boy; but you must also have the school. Strict opportunities and defined hours are the very outline of that enjoyment. A man like Mr. Pickwick has been at school all his life, and when he comes out he astonishes the youngsters. His heart, as that acute psychologist, Mr. Weller, points out, had been born later than his body. It will be remembered that Mr. Pickwick also, when on the escapade of Winkle and Miss Allen, took immoderate pleasure in the performances of a dark lantern which was not dark enough, and was nothing but a nuisance to everybody. His soul also was with Stevenson's boys on the grey sands of Haddington, talking in the dark by the sea. He also was of the league of the "Lantern Bearers."

Stevenson, I remember, says that in the shops of that town they could purchase "penny Pickwicks (that remarkable cigar)." Let us hope they smoked them, and that the rotund ghost of Pickwick hovered over the rings of smoke.

Pickwick goes through life with that god-like gullibility which is the key to all adventures. The greenhorn is the ultimate victor in everything ; it is he that gets the most out of life. Because Pickwick is led away by Jingle, he will be led to the White Hart Inn, and see the only Weller cleaning boots in the courtyard. Because he is bamboozled by Dodson and Fogg, he will enter the prison house like a paladin, and rescue the man and the woman who have wronged him most. His soul will never starve for exploits or excitements who is wise enough to be made a fool of. He will make himself happy in the traps that have been laid for him ; he will roll in their nets and sleep. All doors will fly open to him who has a mildness more defiant than mere courage. The whole is unerringly expressed in one fortunate phrase—he will be always "taken in." To be taken in everywhere is to see the inside of everything. It is the hospitality of circumstance. With torches and trumpets, like a guest, the greenhorn is taken in by Life. And the sceptic is cast out by it.

CHAPTER V

THE GREAT POPULARITY

THERE is one aspect of Charles Dickens which must be of interest even to that subterranean race which does not admire his books. Even if we are not interested in Dickens as a great event in English literature, we must still be interested in him as a great event in English history. If he had not his place with Fielding and Thackeray, he would still have his place with Wat Tyler and Wilkes; for the man led a mob. He did what no English statesman, perhaps, has really done; he called out the people. He was popular in a sense of which we moderns have not even a notion. In that sense there is no popularity now. There are no popular authors to-day. We call such authors as Mr. Guy Boothby or Mr. William Le Queux popular authors. But this is popularity altogether in a weaker sense; not only in quantity, but in quality. The old popularity was positive; the new is negative. There is a great deal of difference between the eager man who wants to read a book, and the tired man who wants a book to read. A man reading a Le Queux mystery wants to get to the end of it. A man reading the Dickens novel wished that it might never end. Men read a Dickens story six times because they knew it so well. If a man can read a Le Queux story six times it is only because he can forget it six times. In short, the Dickens novel was popular, not because it was an unreal world, but because it was a real world; a world in which the soul could live. The modern "shocker" at its very best is an interlude in life. But in the days when Dickens's work was coming out in serial, people talked as if real life were itself the interlude between one issue of "Pickwick" and another.

In reaching the period of the publication of "Pickwick," we reach this sudden apotheosis of Dickens. Henceforward he filled the literary world in a way hard to imagine. Fragments of that huge fashion remain in our daily language; in the talk of every trade or public question are embedded the wrecks of that enormous religion. Men give out the airs of Dickens without even opening his books; just as Catholics can live in a tradition of Christianity without having looked at the New Testament. The man in the street has more memories of Dickens, whom he has not read, than of Marie Corelli, whom he has. There is

nothing in any way parallel to this omnipresence
and vitality in the great comic characters of Boz.
There are no modern Bumbles and Pecksniffs, no
modern Gamps and Micawbers. Mr. Rudyard
Kipling (to take an author of a higher type than
those before mentioned) is called, and called justly,
a popular author; that is to say, he is widely read,
greatly enjoyed, and highly remunerated; he has
achieved the paradox of at once making poetry and
making money.   But let any one who wishes to
see the difference try the experiment of assuming
the Kipling characters to be common property like
the Dickens characters.   Let any one go into an
average parlour and allude to Strickland as he
would allude to Mr. Bumble, the Beadle.   Let any-
one say that somebody is "a perfect Learoyd," as
he would say "a perfect Pecksniff."   Let any one
write a comic paragraph for a halfpenny paper, and
allude to Mrs. Hawksbee instead of to Mrs. Gamp.
He will soon discover that the modern world has
forgotten its own fiercest booms more completely
than it has forgotten this formless tradition from
its fathers.   The mere dregs of it come to more
than any contemporary excitement; the gleaning
of the grapes of "Pickwick" is more than the whole
vintage of "Soldiers Three."   There is one instance,
and I think only one, of an exception to this

generalization; there is one figure in our popular
literature which would really be recognized by the
populace. Ordinary men would understand you if
you referred currently to Sherlock Holmes. Sir
Arthur Conan Doyle would no doubt be justified
in rearing his head to the stars, remembering that
Sherlock Holmes is the only really familiar figure
in modern fiction. But let him droop that head
again with a gentle sadness, remembering that if
Sherlock Holmes is the only familiar figure in
modern fiction, Sherlock Holmes is also the only
familiar figure in the Sherlock Holmes tales. Not
many people could say offhand what was the name
of the owner of Silver Blaze, or whether Mrs.
Watson was dark or fair. But if Dickens had
written the Sherlock Holmes stories, every
character in them would have been equally arresting and memorable. A Sherlock Holmes would
have cooked the dinner for Sherlock Holmes; a
Sherlock Holmes would have driven his cab. If
Dickens brought in a man merely to carry a letter,
he had time for a touch or two, and made him a
giant. Dickens not only conquered the world, he
conquered it with minor characters. Mr. John
Smauker, the servant of Mr. Cyrus Bantam,
though he merely passes across the stage, is almost
as vivid to us as Mr. Samuel Weller, the servant of

Mr. Samuel Pickwick. The young man with the lumpy forehead, who only says "Esker" to Mr. Podsnap's foreign gentleman, is as good as Mr. Podsnap himself. They appear only for a fragment of time, but they belong to eternity. We have them only for an instant, but they have us for ever.

In dealing with Dickens, then, we are dealing with a man whose public success was a marvel and almost a monstrosity. And here I perceive that my friend, the purely artistic critic, primed with Flaubert and Turgenev, can contain himself no longer. He leaps to his feet, upsetting his cup of cocoa, and asks contemptuously what all this has to do with criticism. "Why begin your study of an author," he says, "with trash about popularity? Boothby is popular, and Le Queux is popular, and Mother Siegel is popular. If Dickens was even more popular, it may only mean that Dickens was even worse. The people like bad literature. If your object is to show that Dickens was good literature, you should rather apologize for his popularity, and try to explain it away. You should seek to show that Dickens's work was good literature, although it was popular. Yes, that is your task, to prove that Dickens was admirable, although he was admired!"

I ask the artistic critic to be patient for a little and to believe that I have a serious reason for registering this historic popularity. To that we shall come presently. But as a manner of approach I may perhaps ask leave to examine this actual and fashionable statement, to which I have supposed him to have recourse—the statement that the people likes bad literature, and even likes literature because it is bad. This way of stating the thing is an error, and in that error lies matter of much import to Dickens and his destiny in letters. The public does not like bad literature. The public likes a certain kind of literature and likes that kind of literature even when it is bad better than another kind of literature even when it is good. Nor is this unreasonable ; for the line between different types of literature is as real as the line between tears and laughter; and to tell people who can only get bad comedy that you have some first-class tragedy is as irrational as to offer a man who is shivering over weak warm coffee a really superior sort of ice.

Ordinary people dislike the delicate modern work, not because it is good or because it is bad, but because it is not the thing that they asked for. If, for instance, you find them pent in sterile streets and hungering for adventure and a violent secrecy,

and if you then give them their choice between "A
Study in Scarlet," a good detective story, and
"The Autobiography of Mark Rutherford," a
good psychological monologue, no doubt they
will prefer " A Study in Scarlet." But they will
not do so because "The Autobiography of Mark
Rutherford" is a very good monologue, but because it is evidently a very poor detective story.
They will be indifferent to " Les Aveugles," not
because it is good drama, but because it is bad
melodrama. They do not like good introspective
sonnets ; but neither do they like bad introspective
sonnets, of which there are many. When they
walk behind the brass of the Salvation Army band,
instead of listening to harmonies at Queen's Hall,
it is always assumed that they prefer bad music.
But it may be merely that they prefer military
music, music marching down the open street, and
that if Dan Godfrey's band could be smitten with
salvation and lead them, they would like that even
better. And while they might easily get more
satisfaction out of a screaming article in *The War
Cry* than out of a page of Emerson about the
Oversoul, this would not be because the page of
Emerson is another and superior kind of literature.
It would be because the page of Emerson is
another (and inferior) kind of religion.

Dickens stands first as a defiant monument of
what happens when a great literary genius has a
literary taste akin to that of the community.   For
this kinship was deep and spiritual.   Dickens was
not like our ordinary demagogues and journalists.
Dickens did not write what the people wanted.
Dickens wanted what the people wanted.   And
with this was connected that other fact which must
never be forgotten, and which I have more than
once insisted on, that Dickens and his school had a
hilarious faith in democracy and thought of the
service of it as a sacred priesthood.   Hence there
was this vital point in his popularism, that there
was no condescension in it.   The belief that the
rabble will only read rubbish can be read between
the lines of all our contemporary writers, even of
those writers whose rubbish the rabble reads.   Mr.
Fergus Hume has no more respect for the populace
than Mr. George Moore.   The only difference lies
between those writers who will consent to talk down
to the people, and those writers who will not consent to talk down to the people.   But Dickens never
talked down to the people.   He talked up to the
people.   He approached the people like a deity and
poured out his riches and his blood.   This is what
makes the immortal bond between him and the
masses of men.   He had not merely produced

something they could understand, but he took it
seriously, and toiled and agonized to produce it.
They were not only enjoying one of the best
writers, they were enjoying the best he could do.
His raging and sleepless nights, his wild walks in
the darkness, his note-books crowded, his nerves in
rags, all this extraordinary output was but a fit
sacrifice to the ordinary man. He climbed towards
the lower classes. He panted upwards on weary
wings to reach the heaven of the poor.

His power, then, lay in the fact that he expressed
with an energy and brilliancy quite uncommon the
things close to the common mind. But with this
mere phrase, the common mind, we collide with a
current error. Commonness and the common mind
are now generally spoken of as meaning in some
manner inferiority and the inferior mind; the mind
of the mere mob. But the common mind means
the mind of all the artists and heroes; or else it
would not be common. Plato had the common
mind; Dante had the common mind; or that mind
was not common. Commonness means the quality
common to the saint and the sinner, to the philosopher and the fool; and it was this that Dickens
grasped and developed. In everybody there is a
certain thing that loves babies, that fears death,
that likes sunlight: that thing enjoys Dickens. And

everybody does not mean uneducated crowds;
everybody means everybody : everybody means
Mrs. Meynell. This lady, a cloistered and fastidious
writer, has written one of the best eulogies of
Dickens that exist, an essay in praise of his
pungent perfection of epithet. And when I say
that everybody understands Dickens I do not
mean that he is suited to the untaught intelligence.
I mean that he is so plain that even scholars
can understand him.

The best expression of the fact, however, is to be
found in noting the two things in which he is most
triumphant. In order of artistic value, next after
his humour, comes his horror. And both his
humour and his horror are of a kind strictly to be
called human ; that is, they belong to the basic part
of us, below the lowest roots of our variety. His
horror for instance is a healthy churchyard horror,
a fear of the grotesque defamation called death ;
and this every man has, even if he also has the
more delicate and depraved fears that come of an
evil spiritual outlook. We may be afraid of a
fine shade with Henry James ; that is we may
be afraid of the world. We may be afraid of a taut
silence with Maeterlinck, that is, we may be afraid
of our own souls. But every one will certainly be
afraid of a Cock Lane Ghost, including Henry

James and Maeterlinck.   This latter is literally a
mortal fear, a fear of death ; it is not the immortal
fear, or fear of damnation, which belongs to all the
more refined intellects of our day.   In a word,
Dickens does, in the exact sense, make the flesh
creep ; he does not, like the decadents, make the
soul crawl.   And the creeping of the flesh on being
reminded of its fleshly failure is a strictly universal
thing which we can all feel, while some of us are as
yet uninstructed in the art of spiritual crawling.   In
the same way the Dickens mirth is a part of man
and universal.   All men can laugh at broad humour,
even the subtle humorists.   Even the modern
flâneur, who can smile at a particular combination
of green and yellow, would laugh at Mr. Lammle's
request for Mr. Fledgeby's nose.   In a word—the
common things are common—even to the uncommon people.

These two primary dispositions of Dickens,
to make the flesh creep and to make the sides
ache were a sort of twins of his spirit; they
were never far apart and the fact of their
affinity is interestingly exhibited in the first two
novels.

Generally he mixed the two up in a book and
mixed a great many other things with them.   As
a rule he cared little if he kept six stories of quite

different colours running in the same book. The effect was sometimes similar to that of playing six tunes at once. He does not mind the coarse tragic figure of Jonas Chuzzlewit crossing the mental stage which is full of the allegorical pantomime of Eden, Mr. Chollop and the *Watertoast Gazette*, a scene which is as much of a satire as "Gulliver," and nearly as much of a fairy tale. He does not mind binding up a rather pompous sketch of prostitution in the same book with an adorable impossibility like Bunsby. But "Pickwick" is so far a coherent thing that it is coherently comic and consistently rambling. And as a consequence his next book was, upon the whole, coherently and consistently horrible. As his natural turn for terrors was kept down in "Pickwick," so his natural turn for joy and laughter is kept down in "Oliver Twist." In "Oliver Twist" the smoke of the thieves' kitchen hangs over the whole tale, and the shadow of Fagin falls everywhere. The little lamp-lit rooms of Mr. Brownlow and Rose Maylie are to all appearance purposely kept subordinate, a mere foil to the foul darkness without. It was a strange and appropriate accident that Cruikshank and not "Phiz" should have illustrated this book. There was about Cruikshank's art a kind of cramped energy which is almost the definition of the criminal mind. His drawings have a dark strength: yet he does not only draw morbidly, he draws meanly. In the doubled-up figure and frightful eyes of Fagin in the condemned cell there is not only a baseness of subject; there is a kind of baseness in the very technique of it. It is not drawn with the free lines of a free man; it has the half-witted secrecies of a hunted thief. It does not look merely like a picture of Fagin; it looks like a picture by Fagin. Among these dark and detestable plates there is one which has with a kind of black directness, the dreadful poetry that does inhere in the story, stumbling as it often is. It represents Oliver asleep at an open window in the house of one of his humaner patrons. And outside the window, but as big and close as if they were in the room stand Fagin and the foul-faced Monk, staring at him with dark monstrous visages and great white wicked eyes, in the style of the simple devilry of the draughtsman. The very *naïveté* of the horror is horrifying: the very woodenness of the two wicked men seems to make them worse than mere men who are wicked. But this picture of big devils at the window-sill does express, as has been suggested above, the thread of poetry in the whole thing; the sense, that is, of the thieves as a kind of army of devils compassing

earth and sky crying for Oliver's soul and besieging
the house in which he is barred for safety. In
this matter there is, I think, a difference between
the author and the illustrator. In Cruikshank
there was surely something morbid; but, sensitive
and sentimental as Dickens was, there was nothing
morbid in him. He had, as Stevenson had, more
of the mere boy's love of suffocating stories of
blood and darkness; of skulls, of gibbets, of all the
things, in a word, that are sombre without being sad.
There is a ghastly joy in remembering our boyish
reading about Sikes and his flight; especially about
the voice of that unbearable pedlar which went
on in a monotonous and maddening sing-song,
"will wash out grease-stains, mud-stains, blood-
stains," until Sikes fled almost screaming. For
this boyish mixture of appetite and repugnance
there is a good popular phrase, "supping on
horrors." Dickens supped on horrors as he supped
on Christmas pudding. He supped on horrors
because he was an optimist and could sup on
anything. There was no saner or simpler schoolboy than Traddles, who covered all his books with
skeletons.

"Oliver Twist" had begun in Bentley's *Mis-
cellany*, which Dickens edited in 1837. It was
interrupted by a blow that for the moment broke

the author's spirit and seemed to have broken
his heart. His wife's sister, Mary Hogarth died
suddenly. To Dickens his wife's family seems to
have been like his own; his affections were heavily
committed to the sisters, and of this one he was
peculiarly fond. All his life, through much conceit
and sometimes something bordering on selfishness,
we can feel the redeeming note of an almost tragic
tenderness; he was a man who could really have
died of love or sorrow. He took up the work of
"Oliver Twist" again later in the year, and finished
it at the end of 1838. His work was incessant
and almost bewildering. In 1838 he had already
brought out the first number of "Nicholas
Nickleby." But the great popularity went boom-
ing on; the whole world was roaring for books by
Dickens, and more books by Dickens, and Dickens
was labouring night and day like a factory. Among
other things he edited the "Memoirs of Grimaldi."
The incident is only worth mentioning for the
sake of one more example of the silly ease with
which Dickens was drawn by criticism and the
clever ease with which he managed, in these small
squabbles, to defend himself. Somebody mildly
suggested that, after all, Dickens had never known
Grimaldi. Dickens was down on him like a
thunderbolt, sardonically asking how close an

intimacy Lord Braybrooke had with Mr. Samuel Pepys.

"Nicholas Nickleby" is the most typical perhaps of the tone of his earlier works. It is in form a very rambling, old-fashioned romance, the kind of romance in which the hero is only a convenience for the frustration of the villain. Nicholas is what is called in theatricals a stick. But any stick is good enough to beat a Squeers with. That strong thwack, that simplified energy is the whole object of such a story; and the whole of this tale is full of a kind of highly picturesque platitude. The wicked aristocrats, Sir Mulberry Hawk, Lord Verisopht and the rest are inadequate versions of the fashionable profligate. But this is not (as some suppose) because Dickens in his vulgarity could not comprehend the refinement of patrician vice. There is no idea more vulgar or more ignorant than the notion that a gentleman is generally what is called refined. The error of the Hawk conception is that, if anything, he is too refined. Real aristocratic blackguards do not swagger and rant so well. A real fast baronet would not have defied Nicholas in the tavern with so much oratorical dignity. A real fast baronet would probably have been choked with apoplectic embarrassment and said nothing at all. But Dickens read into this aristocracy a grandiloquence and a natural poetry which, like all melodrama, is really the precious jewel of the poor.

But the book contains something which is much more Dickensian. It is exquisitely characteristic of Dickens that the truly great achievement of the story is the person who delays the story. Mrs. Nickleby, with her beautiful mazes of memory, does her best to prevent the story of Nicholas Nickleby from being told. And she does well. There is no particular necessity that we should know what happens to Madeline Bray. There is a desperate and crying necessity that we should know that Mrs. Nickleby once had a foot-boy who had a wart on his nose and a driver who had a green shade over his left eye. If Mrs. Nickleby is a fool, she is one of those fools who are wiser than the world. She stands for a great truth which we must not forget; the truth that experience is not in real life a saddening thing at all. The people who have had misfortunes are generally the people who love to talk about them. Experience is really one of the gaieties of old age, one of its dissipations. Mere memory becomes a kind of debauch. Experience may be disheartening to those who are foolish enough to try to co-ordinate it and to draw deductions from it. But to those happy souls, like Mrs. Nickleby, to whom relevancy is nothing, the whole of their past life is like an inexhaustible fairyland. Just as we take a rambling walk because we know that a whole district is beautiful, so they indulge a rambling mind because they know that a whole existence is interesting. A boy does not plunge into his future more romantically and at random, than they plunge into their past.

Another gleam in the book is Mr. Mantalini. Of him, as of all the really great comic characters of Dickens, it is impossible to speak with any critical adequacy. Perfect absurdity is a direct thing, like physical pain, or a strong smell. A joke is a fact. However indefensible it is it cannot be attacked. However defensible it is it cannot be defended. That Mr. Mantalini should say in praising the " outline " of his wife, " The two Countesses had no outlines, and the Dowager's was a demd outline,"—this can only be called an unanswerable absurdity. You may try to analyse it, as Charles Lamb did the indefensible joke about the hare ; you may dwell for a moment on the dark distinctions between the negative disqualification of the Countess and the positive disqualification of the Dowager, but you will not capture the violent beauty of it in any way. " She will be a lovely widow. I shall be a body. Some handsome women

will cry; she will laugh demnebly." This vision
of demoniac heartlessness has the same defiant
finality. I mention the matter here, but it has
to be remembered in connection with all the comic
masterpieces of Dickens. Dickens has greatly
suffered with the critics precisely through this
stunning simplicity in his best work. The critic
is called upon to describe his sensations while
enjoying Mantalini and Micawber, and he can no
more describe them than he can describe a blow
in the face. Thus Dickens, in this self-conscious,
analytical and descriptive age, loses both ways.
He is doubly unfitted for the best modern criticism.
His bad work is below that criticism. His good
work is above it.

But gigantic as were Dickens's labours, gigantic
as were the exactions from him, his own plans
were more gigantic still. He had the type of mind
that wishes to do every kind of work at once; to
do everybody's work as well as its own. There
floated before him a vision of a monstrous magazine, entirely written by himself. It is true that
when this scheme came to be discussed, he suggested that other pens might be occasionally
employed; but, reading between the lines, it is
sufficiently evident that he thought of the thing
as a kind of vast multiplication of himself, with

Dickens as editor opening letters, Dickens as leader-writer writing leaders, Dickens as reporter reporting meetings, Dickens as reviewer reviewing books, Dickens, for all I know, as office-boy opening and shutting doors.   This serial, of which he spoke to Messrs. Chapman and Hall, began and broke off and remains as a colossal fragment bound together under the title of "Master Humphrey's Clock."   One characteristic thing he wished to have in the periodical.   He suggested an Arabian Nights of London, in which Gog and Magog, the giants of the city, should give forth chronicles as enormous as themselves.   He had a taste for these schemes or frameworks for many tales.   He made and abandoned many; many he half-fulfilled.   I strongly suspect that he meant Major Jackman, in "Mrs. Lirriper's Lodgings" and "Mrs. Lirriper's Legacy," to start a series of studies of that lady's lodgers, a kind of history of No. 81, Norfolk Street, Strand.   "The Seven Poor Travellers" was planned for seven stories; we will not say seven poor stories.   Dickens had meant, probably, to write a tale for each article of "Somebody's Luggage:" he only got as far as the hat and the boots.   This gigantesque scale of literary architecture, huge and yet curiously cosy, is characteristic of his spirit, fond of size and yet fond of comfort.   He liked to

have story within story, like room within room
of some labyrinthine but comfortable castle.   In
this spirit he wished " Master Humphrey's Clock "
to begin, and to be a big frame or bookcase for
numberless novels.   The clock started ; but the
clock stopped.

In the prologue by Master Humphrey reappear
Mr. Pickwick and Sam Weller, and of that resurrec-
tion many things have been said, chiefly expressions of a reasonable regret.   Doubtless they do
not add much to their author's reputation, but they
add a great deal to their author's pleasure.   It was
ingrained in him to wish to meet old friends.   All
his characters are, so to speak, designed to be old
friends ; in a sense every Dickens character is an
old friend, even when he first appears.   He comes
to us mellow out of many implied interviews, and
carries the firelight on his face.   Dickens was simply
pleased to meet Pickwick again, and being pleased,
he made the old man too comfortable to be amusing.

But "Master Humphrey's Clock" is now scarcely
known except as the shell of one of the well-known
novels.   " The Old Curiosity Shop " was published
in accordance with the original "Clock" scheme.
Perhaps the most typical thing about it is the title.
There seems no reason in particular, at the first
and most literal glance, why the story should be

called after the Old Curiosity Shop. Only two of
the characters have anything to do with such a
shop, and they leave it for ever in the first few
pages. It is as if Thackeray had called the whole
novel of "Vanity Fair" "Miss Pinkerton's Academy."
It is as if Scott had given the whole story of "The
Antiquary" the title of "The Hawes Inn." But
when we feel the situation with more fidelity we
realize that this title is something in the nature of a
key to the whole Dickens romance. His tales always
started from some splendid hint in the streets.
And shops, perhaps the most poetical of all things,
often set off his fancy galloping. Every shop, in
fact, was to him the door of romance. Among
all the huge serial schemes of which we have spoken,
it is a matter of wonder that he never started an
endless periodical called "The Street," and divided
it into shops. He could have written an exquisite
romance called "The Baker's Shop;" another
called "The Chemist's Shop;" another called "The
Oil Shop," to keep company with "The Old
Curiosity Shop." Some incomparable baker he
invented and forgot. Some gorgeous chemist
might have been. Some more than mortal oil-man
is lost to us for ever. This Old Curiosity Shop
he did happen to linger by : its tale he did happen
to tell.

Around "Little Nell," of course, a controversy
raged and rages; some implored Dickens not to
kill her at the end of the story : some regret that
he did not kill her at the beginning. To me the
chief interest in this young person lies in the
fact that she is an example, and the most celebrated example of what must have been, I think,
a personal peculiarity, perhaps a personal experience of Dickens. There is, of course, no
paradox at all in saying that if we find in a good
book a wildly impossible character it is very
probable indeed that it was copied from a real
person. This is one of the common-places of good
art criticism. For although people talk of the
restraints of fact and the freedom of fiction, the
case for most artistic purposes is quite the other
way. Nature is as free as air : art is forced to look
probable. There may be a million things that do
happen, and yet only one thing that convinces us
as likely to happen. Out of a million possible
things there may be only one appropriate thing.
I fancy, therefore, that many stiff, unconvincing
characters are copied from the wild freak-show of
real life. And in many parts of Dickens's work
there is evidence of some peculiar affection on his
part for a strange sort of little girl; a little girl
with a premature sense of responsibility and duty ;

a sort of saintly precocity. Did he know some
little girl of this kind? Did she die, perhaps, and
remain in his memory in colours too ethereal and
pale? In any case there are a great number of
them in his works. Little Dorrit was one of them,
and Florence Dombey with her brother, and even
Agnes in infancy; and, of course, Little Nell. And,
in any case, one thing is evident; whatever charm
these children may have they have not the charm
of childhood. They are not little children: they
are "little mothers." The beauty and divinity in
a child lie in his not being worried, not being
conscientious, not being like Little Nell. Little
Nell has never, any of the sacred bewilderment
of a baby. She never wears that face, beautiful
but almost half-witted, with which a real child
half understands that there is evil in the universe.

As usual, however, little as the story has to do
with the title, the splendid and satisfying pages
have even less to do with the story. Dick Swiveller is perhaps the noblest of all the noble creations of Dickens. He has all the overwhelming
absurdity of Mantalini, with the addition of being
human and credible, for he knows he is absurd.
His high-falutin is not done because he seriously
thinks it right and proper, like that of Mr. Snod-
grass, nor is it done because he thinks it will serve

his turn, like that of Mr. Pecksniff, for both these
beliefs are improbable; it is done because he really
loves high-falutin, because he has a lonely literary
pleasure in exaggerative language. Great draughts
of words are to him like great draughts of wine—
pungent and yet refreshing, light and yet leaving
him in a glow. In unerring instinct for the perfect
folly of a phrase he has no equal, even among the
giants of Dickens. "I am sure," says Miss
Wackles, when she had been flirting with Cheggs,
the market-gardener, and reduced Mr. Swiveller to
Byronic renunciation, "I am sure I'm very sorry
if——" "Sorry," said Mr. Swiveller, "sorry in
the possession of a Cheggs!" The abyss of bitterness is unfathomable. Scarcely less precious is
the pose of Mr. Swiveller when he imitates the
stage brigand. After crying, "Some wine here!
Ho!" he hands the flagon to himself with profound
humility, and receives it haughtily. Perhaps the
very best scene in the book is that between Mr.
Swiveller and the single gentleman with whom he
endeavours to remonstrate for having remained in
bed all day: "We cannot have single gentlemen
coming into the place and sleeping like double
gentlemen without paying extra. . . . An equal
amount of slumber was never got out of one bed,
and if you want to sleep like that you must pay for

a double-bedded room." His relations with the
Marchioness are at once purely romantic and
purely genuine; there is nothing even of Dickens's
legitimate exaggerations about them.   A shabby,
larky, good-natured clerk would, as a matter of
fact, spend hours in the society of a little servant
girl if he found her about the house.   It would
arise partly from a dim kindliness, and partly from
that mysterious instinct which is sometimes called,
mistakenly, a love of low company—that mysterious instinct which makes so many men of pleasure find something soothing in the society of
uneducated people, particularly uneducated women.
It is the instinct which accounts for the otherwise
unaccountable popularity of barmaids.

And still the pot of that huge popularity boiled.
In 1841 another novel was demanded, and "Barnaby
Rudge" supplied.   It is chiefly of interest as an
embodiment of that other element in Dickens, the
picturesque or even the pictorial.   Barnaby Rudge,
the idiot with his rags and his feathers and his
raven, the bestial hangman, the blind mob—all
make a picture, though they hardly make a novel.
One touch there is in it of the richer and more
humorous Dickens, the boy-conspirator, Mr. Sim
Tappertit.   But he might have been treated with
more sympathy—with as much sympathy, for

instance, as Mr. Dick Swiveller; for he is only the
romantic guttersnipe, the bright boy at the particular age when it is most fascinating to found a
secret society and most difficult to keep a secret.
And if ever there was a romantic guttersnipe on
earth it was Charles Dickens. " Barnaby Rudge "
is no more an historical novel than Sim's secret
league was a political movement; but they are both
beautiful creations.   When all is said, however, the
main reason for mentioning the work here is that it
is the next bubble in the pot, the next thing that
burst out of that whirling, seething head.   The tide
of it rose and smoked and sang till it boiled over
the pot of Britain and poured over all America.
In the January of 1842 he set out for the United
States.

CHAPTER VI

DICKENS AND AMERICA

THE essential of Dickens's character was the conjunction of common sense with uncommon sensibility. The two things are not, indeed, in such an antithesis as is commonly imagined. Great English literary authorities, such as Jane Austen and Mr. Chamberlain, have put the word "sense" and the word "sensibility" in a kind of opposition to each other. But not only are they not opposite words: they are actually the same word. They both mean receptiveness or approachability by the facts outside us. To have a sense of colour is the same as to have a sensibility to colour. A person who realizes that beef-steaks are appetizing shows his sensibility. A person who realizes that moonrise is romantic shows his sense. But it is not difficult to see the meaning and need of the popular distinction between sensibility and sense, particularly in the form called common sense. Common sense is a sensibility duly distributed in all normal directions; sensibility has come to mean a specialized sensibility in one.

This is unfortunate, for it is not the sensibility that is bad, but the specializing; that is, the lack of sensibility to everything else. A young lady who stays out all night to look at the stars should not be blamed for her sensibility to starlight, but for her insensibility to other people. A poet who recites his own verses from ten to five with the tears rolling down his face should decidedly be rebuked for his lack of sensibility—his lack of sensibility to those grand rhythms of the social harmony, crudely called manners. For all politeness is a long poem, since it is full of recurrences. This balance of all the sensibilities we call sense; and it is in this capacity that it becomes of great importance as an attribute of the character of Dickens.

Dickens, I repeat, had common sense and uncommon sensibility. That is to say, the proportion of interests in him was about the same as that of an ordinary man, but he felt all of them more excitedly. This is a distinction not easy for us to keep in mind, because we hear to-day chiefly of two types, the dull man who likes ordinary things mildly, and the extraordinary man who likes extraordinary things wildly. But Dickens liked quite ordinary things; he merely made an extraordinary fuss about them. His excitement was sometimes like an epileptic fit; but it must not be confused with the fury of the man of one idea or one line of ideas. He had the excess of the eccentric, but not the defects, the narrowness. Even when he raved like a maniac he did not rave like a monomaniac. He had no particular spot of sensibility or spot of insensibility : he was merely a normal man minus a normal self-command. He had no special point of mental pain or repugnance, like Ruskin's horror of steam and iron, or Mr. Bernard Shaw's permanent irritation against romantic love. He was annoyed at the ordinary annoyances : only he was more annoyed than was necessary. He did not desire strange delights, blue wine or black women with Baudelaire, or cruel sights east of Suez with Mr. Kipling. He wanted what a healthy man wants, only he was ill with wanting it. To understand him, in a word, we must keep well in mind the medical distinction between delicacy and disease. Perhaps we shall comprehend it and him more clearly if we think of a woman rather than a man. There was much that was feminine about Dickens, and nothing more so than this abnormal normality. A woman is often, in comparison with a man, at once more sensitive and more sane.

This distinction must be especially remembered in all his quarrels. And it must be most especially remembered in what may be called his great quarrel

with America, which we have now to approach.
The whole incident is so typical of Dickens's attitude to everything and anything, and especially of
Dickens's attitude to anything political, that I may
ask permission to approach the matter by another,
a somewhat long and curving avenue.

Common sense is a fairy thread, thin and faint,
and as easily lost as gossamer. Dickens (in large
matters) never lost it. Take, as an example, his
political tone or drift throughout his life. His
views, of course, may have been right or wrong;
the reforms he supported may have been successful
or otherwise: that is not a matter for this book.
But if we compare him with the other men that
wanted the same things (or the other men that
wanted the other things) we feel a startling absence
of cant, a startling sense of humanity as it is, and
of the eternal weakness. He was a fierce democrat,
but in his best vein he laughed at the cocksure
Radical of common life, the red-faced man who
said, "Prove it!" when anybody said anything.
He fought for the right to elect: but he would not
whitewash elections. He believed in Parliamentary
government; but he did not, like our contemporary
newspapers, pretend that Parliament is something
much more heroic and imposing than it is. He
fought for the rights of the grossly oppressed

Nonconformists ; but he spat out of his mouth the
unction of that too easy seriousness with which
they oiled everything, and held up to them like
a horrible mirror the foul fat face of Chadband.
He saw that Mr. Podsnap thought too little of
places outside England. But he saw that Mrs.
Jellaby thought too much of them. In the last
book he wrote he gives us, in Mr. Honeythunder,
a hateful and wholesome picture of all the Liberal
catchwords pouring out of one illiberal man. But
perhaps the best evidence of this steadiness and
sanity is the fact that, dogmatic as he was, he never
tied himself to any passing dogma : he never got
into any *cul de sac* of civic or economic fanaticism :
he went down the broad road of the Revolution.
He never admitted that economically, we must
make hells of workhouses, any more than Rousseau
would have admitted it. He never said the State
had no right to teach children or save their bones,
any more than Danton would have said it. He
was a fierce Radical ; but he was never a Man-
chester Radical. He used the test of Utility, but
he was never a Utilitarian. While economists
were writing soft words he wrote " Hard Times,"
which Macaulay called " sullen Socialism," because
it was not complacent Whiggism. But Dickens
was never a Socialist any more than he was an

Individualist; and, whatever else he was, he certainly was not sullen. He was not even a politician of any kind. He was simply a man of very clear, airy judgment on things that did not inflame his private temper, and he perceived that any theory that tried to run the living State entirely on one force and motive was probably nonsense. Whenever the Liberal philosophy had embedded in it something hard and heavy and lifeless, by an instinct he dropped it out. He was too romantic, perhaps, but he would have to do only with real things. He may have cared too much about Liberty. But he cared nothing about "*Laissez Faire.*"

Now, among many interests of his contact with America this interest emerges as infinitely the largest and most striking, that it gave a final example of this queer, unexpected coolness and candour of his, this abrupt and sensational rationality. Apart altogether from any question of the accuracy of his picture of America, the American indignation was particularly natural and inevitable. For the large circumstances of the age must be taken into account. At the end of the previous epoch the whole of our Christian civilization had been startled from its sleep by trumpets to take sides in a bewildering Armageddon, often with eyes

still misty. Germany and Austria found themselves on the side of the old order, France and
America on the side of the new. England, as at
the Reformation, took up eventually a dark middle
position, maddeningly difficult to define. She
created a democracy, but she kept an aristocracy :
she reformed the House of Commons, but left the
magistracy (as it is still) a mere league of gentlemen
against the world. But underneath all this doubt
and compromise there was in England a great and
perhaps growing mass of dogmatic democracy ;
certainly thousands, probably millions expected a
Republic in fifty years. And for these the first
instinct was obvious. The first instinct was to
look across the Atlantic to where lay a part of
ourselves already Republican, the van of the advancing English on the road to liberty. Nearly all
the great Liberals of the nineteenth century enormously idealized America. On the other hand, to
the Americans, fresh from their first epic of arms,
the defeated mother country, with its coronets and
county magistrates, was only a broken feudal keep.

So much is self-evident. But nearly halfway
through the nineteenth century there came out of
England the voice of a violent satirist. In its
political quality it seemed like the half-choked cry
of the frustrated republic. It had no patience with

the pretence that England was already free, that we
had gained all that was valuable from the Revolution.   It poured a cataract of contempt on the so-
called working compromises of England, on the
oligarchic cabinets, on the two artificial parties, on
the government offices, on the J.P.'s, on the vestries,
on the voluntary charities.   This satirist was
Dickens, and it must be remembered that he was
not only fierce, but uproariously readable.   He
really damaged the things he struck at, a very
rare thing.   He stepped up to the grave official of
the vestry, really trusted by the rulers, really feared
like a god by the poor, and he tied round his neck
a name that choked him; never again now can he
be anything but Bumble.   He confronted the fine
old English gentleman who gives his patriotic
services for nothing as a local magistrate, and he
nailed him up as Nupkins, an owl in open day.
For to this satire there is literally no answer; it
cannot be denied that a man like Nupkins can be
and is a magistrate, so long as we adopt the amazing
method of letting the rich man of a district actually
be the judge in it.   We can only avoid the vision
of the fact by shutting our eyes, and imagining the
nicest rich man we can think of; and that, of course,
is what we do.   But Dickens, in this matter, was
merely realistic; he merely asked us to look on

Nupkins, on the wild, strange thing that we had made. Thus Dickens seemed to see England not at all as the country where freedom slowly broadened down from precedent to precedent, but as a rubbish heap of seventeeth-century bad habits abandoned by everybody else. That is, he looked at England almost with the eyes of an American democrat.

And so, when the voice, swelling in volume, reached America and the Americans, the Americans said, "Here is a man who will hurry the old country along, and tip her kings and beadles into the sea. Let him come here, and we will show him a race of free men such as he dreams of, alive upon the ancient earth. Let him come here and tell the English of the divine democracy towards which he drives them. There he has a monarchy and an oligarchy to make game of. Here is a republic for him to praise." It seemed, indeed, a very natural sequel, that having denounced undemocratic England as the wilderness, he should announce democratic America as the promised land. Any ordinary person would have prophesied that as he had pushed his rage at the old order almost to the edge of rant, he would push his encomium of the new order almost to the edge of cant. Amid a roar of republican idealism, compliments, hope, and anticipatory gratitude, the great democrat entered the great democracy. He looked about him; he saw a complete America, unquestionably progressive, unquestionably self-governing. Then, with a more than American coolness, and a more than American impudence, he sat down and wrote "Martin Chuzzlewit." That tricky and perverse sanity of his had mutinied again. Common sense is a wild thing, savage, and beyond rules; and it had turned on them and rent them.

The main course of action was as follows; and it is right to record it before we speak of the justice of it. When I speak of his sitting down and writing "Martin Chuzzlewit," I use, of course, an elliptical expression. He wrote the notes of the American part of "Martin Chuzzlewit" while he was still in America; but it was a later decision presumably that such impressions should go into a book, and it was little better than an afterthought that they should go into "Martin Chuzzlewit." Dickens had an uncommonly bad habit (artistically speaking) of altering a story in the middle as he did in the case of "Our Mutual Friend." And it is on record that he only sent young Martin to America because he did not know what else to do with him, and because (to say truth) the sales were falling off. But the first action, which Americans

regarded as an equally hostile one, was the publication of "American Notes," the history of which
should first be given. His notion of visiting
America had come to him as a very vague notion,
even before the appearance of "The Old Curiosity
Shop." But it had grown in him through the
whole ensuing period in the plaguing and per-
sistent way that ideas did grow in him and live
with him. He contended against the idea in a
certain manner. He had much to induce him to
contend against it. Dickens was by this time not
only a husband, but a father, the father of several
children, and their existence made a difficulty in
itself. His wife, he said, cried whenever the project was mentioned. But it was a point in him that
he could never, with any satisfaction, part with a
project. He had that restless optimism, that kind
of nervous optimism, which would always tend to
say "Yes"; which is stricken with an immortal
repentance, if ever it says "No." The idea of
seeing America might be doubtful, but the idea
of not seeing America was dreadful. "To miss
this opportunity would be a sad thing," he says.
". . . God willing, I think it *must* be managed
somehow!" It was managed somehow. First of
all he wanted to take his children as well as his
wife. Final obstacles to this fell upon him, but

they did not frustrate him. A serious illness fell on him; but that did not frustrate him. He sailed for America in 1842.

He landed in America, and he liked it. As John Forster very truly says, it is due to him, as well as to the great country that welcomed him, that his first good impression should be recorded, and that it should be "considered independently of any modification it afterwards underwent." But the modification it afterwards underwent was, as I have said above, simply a sudden kicking against cant, that is, against repetition. He was quite ready to believe that all Americans were free men. He would have believed it if they had not all told him so. He was quite prepared to be pleased with America. He would have been pleased with it if it had not been so much pleased with itself. The "modification" his view underwent did not arise from any modification of America as he first saw it. His admiration did not change because America changed. It changed because America did not change. The Yankees enraged him at last, not by saying different things, but by saying the same things. They were a republic; they were a new and vigorous nation; it seemed natural that they should say so to a famous foreigner first stepping on to their shore. But it seemed maddening that they should say so to each other in every car and drinking saloon from morning till night. It was not that the Americans in any way ceased from praising him. It was rather that they went on praising him. It was not merely that their praises of him sounded beautiful when he first heard them. Their praises of themselves sounded beautiful when he first heard them. That democracy was grand, and that Charles Dickens was a remarkable person, were two truths that he certainly never doubted to his dying day. But, as I say, it was a soulless repetition that stung his sense of humour out of sleep; it woke like a wild beast for hunting, the lion of his laughter. He had heard the truth once too often. He had heard the truth for the nine hundred and ninety-ninth time, and he suddenly saw that it was falsehood.

It is true that a particular circumstance sharpened and defined his disappointment. He felt very hotly, as he felt everything, whether selfish or unselfish, the injustice of the American piracies of English literature, resulting from the American copyright laws. He did not go to America with any idea of discussing this; when, some time afterwards, somebody said that he did, he violently rejected the view as only describable "in one of the shortest words in the English

language." But his entry into America was almost
triumphal; the rostrum or pulpit was ready for
him; he felt strong enough to say anything. He
had been most warmly entertained by many
American men of letters, especially by Washington
Irving, and in his consequent glow of confidence
he stepped up to the dangerous question of American copyright. He made many speeches attacking
the American law and theory of the matter as
unjust to English writers and to American readers.
The effect appears to have astounded him. "I
believe there is no country," he writes, "on the
face of the earth where there is less freedom of
opinion on any subject in reference to which there
is a broad difference of opinion than in this.
There! I write the words with reluctance, disappointment, and sorrow; but I believe it from
the bottom of my soul. . . . The notion that I, a
man alone by myself in America, should venture
to suggest to the Americans that there was one
point on which they were neither just to their own
countrymen nor to us, actually struck the boldest
dumb! Washington Irving, Prescott, Hoffman,
Bryant, Halleck, Dana, Washington Allston—every
man who writes in this country is devoted to the
question, and not one of them *dares* to raise his
voice and complain of the atrocious state of the

law. . . . The wonder is that a breathing man can
be found with temerity enough to suggest to the
Americans the possibility of their having done
wrong.   I wish you could have seen the faces that
I saw down both sides of the table at Hartford
when I began to talk about Scott.   I wish you
could have heard how I gave it out.   My blood so
boiled when I thought of the monstrous injustice
that I felt as if I were twelve feet high when I
thrust it down their throats."

That is almost a portrait of Dickens. We can
almost see the erect little figure, its face and hair
like a flame.

For such reasons, among others, Dickens was
angry with America. But if America was angry
with Dickens, there were also reasons for it.   I
do not think that the rage against his copyright
speeches was, as he supposed, merely national
insolence and self-satisfaction. America is a
mystery to any good Englishman; but I think
Dickens managed somehow to touch it on a queer
nerve.   There is one thing, at any rate, that must
strike all Englishmen who have the good fortune
to have American friends ; that is, that while there
is no materialism so crude or so material as American materialism, there is also no idealism so crude
or so ideal as American idealism. America will

always affect an Englishman as being soft in the wrong place and hard in the wrong place; coarse exactly where all civilized men are delicate, delicate exactly where all grown-up men are coarse. Some beautiful ideal runs through this people, but it runs aslant. The only existing picture in which the thing I mean has been embodied is in Stevenson's "Wrecker," in the blundering delicacy of Jim Pinkerton. America has a new delicacy, a coarse, rank refinement. But there is another way of embodying the idea, and that is to say this—that nothing is more likely than that the Americans thought it very shocking in Dickens, the divine author, to talk about being done out of money. Nothing would be more American than to expect a genius to be too high-toned for trade. It is certain that they deplored his selfishness in the matter; it is probable that they deplored his indelicacy. A beautiful young dreamer, with flowing brown hair, ought not to be even conscious of his copyrights. For it is quite unjust to say that the Americans worship the dollar. They really do worship intellect—another of the passing superstitions of our time.

If America had then this Pinkertonian propriety, this new, raw sensibility, Dickens was the man to rasp it. He was its precise opposite in every way.

The decencies he did respect were old-fashioned and fundamental. On top of these he had that lounging liberty and comfort which can only be had on the basis of very old conventions, like the carelessness of gentlemen and the deliberation of rustics. He had no fancy for being strung up to that taut and quivering ideality demanded by American patriots and public speakers. And there was something else also, connected especially with the question of copyright and his own pecuniary claims. Dickens was not in the least desirous of being thought too "high-souled" to want his wages, nor was he in the least ashamed of asking for them. Deep in him (whether the modern reader likes the quality or no) was a sense very strong in the old Radicals—very strong especially in the old English Radicals—a sense of personal *rights*, one's own rights included, as something not merely useful but sacred. He did not think a claim any less just and solemn because it happened to be selfish; he did not divide claims into selfish and unselfish, but into right and wrong. It is significant that when he asked for his money, he never asked for it with that shamefaced cynicism, that sort of embarrassed brutality, with which the modern man of the world mutters something about business being business or looking after number

one. He asked for his money in a valiant and
ringing voice, like a man asking for his honour.
While his American critics were moaning and sneer-
ing at his interested motives as a disqualification,
he brandished his interested motives like a banner.
" It is nothing to them," he cries in astonishment,
" that, of all men living, I am the greatest loser by
it " (the Copyright Law). " It is nothing that I have
a claim to speak and be heard." The thing they
set up as a barrier he actually presents as a pass-
port. They think that he, of all men, ought not to
speak because he is interested. He thinks that he,
of all men, ought to speak because he is wronged.

But this particular disappointment with America
in the matter of the tyranny of its public opinion
was not merely the expression of the fact that
Dickens was a typical Englishman ; that is, a man
with a very sharp insistence upon individual
freedom. It also worked back ultimately to that
larger and vaguer disgust of which I have spoken
—the disgust at the perpetual posturing of the
people before a mirror. The tyranny was irritating,
not so much because of the suffering it inflicted on
the minority, but because of the awful glimpses
that it gave of the huge and imbecile happiness of
the majority. The very vastness of the vain race
enraged him, its immensity, its unity, its peace.

He was annoyed more with its contentment than with any of its discontents. The thought of that unthinkable mass of millions, every one of them saying that Washington was the greatest man on earth, and that the Queen lived in the Tower of London, rode his riotous fancy like a nightmare. But to the end he retained the outlines of his original republican ideal and lamented over America not as being too Liberal, but as not being Liberal enough. Among others, he used these somewhat remarkable words: "I tremble for a Radical coming here, unless he is a Radical on principle, by reason and reflection, and from the sense of right. I fear that if he were anything else he would return home a Tory. . . . I say no more on that head for two months from this time, save that I do fear that the heaviest blow ever dealt at liberty will be dealt by this country, in the failure of its example on the earth."

We are still waiting to see if that prediction has been fulfilled; but nobody can say that it has been falsified.

He went west on the great canals; he went south and touched the region of slavery; he saw America superficially indeed, but as a whole. And the great mass of his experience was certainly pleasant, though he vibrated with anticipatory

passion against slave-holders, though he swore
he would accept no public tribute in the slave
country (a resolve which he broke under the
pressure of the politeness of the south), yet his
actual collisions with slavery and its upholders
were few and brief. In these he bore himself
with his accustomed vivacity and fire, but it
would be a great mistake to convey the impression that his mental reaction against America was
chiefly, or even largely, due to his horror at the
negro problem.   Over and above the cant of which
we have spoken, the weary rush of words, the
chief complaint he made was a complaint against
bad manners ; and on a large view his anti-Ameri-
canism would seem to be more founded on spitting
than on slavery. When, however, it did happen
that the primary morality of man-owning came up
for discussion, Dickens displayed an honourable
impatience.   One man, full of anti-abolitionist
ardour, button-holed him and bombarded him with
the well-known argument in defence of slavery,
that it was not to the financial interest of a slave-
owner to damage or weaken his own slaves.
Dickens, in telling the story of this interview,
writes as follows: " I told him quietly that it was
not a man's interest to get drunk, or to steal, or to
game, or to indulge in any other vice; but he *did*

indulge in it for all that. That cruelty and the
abuse of irresponsible power were two of the bad
passions of human nature, with the gratification of
which considerations of interest or of ruin had
nothing whatever to do. . . ." It is hardly possible to doubt that Dickens, in telling the man this,
told him something sane and logical and unanswerable. But it is perhaps permissible to doubt
whether he told it to him quietly.

He returned home in the spring of 1842, and in
the later part of the year his " American Notes " appeared, and the cry against him that had begun over
copyright swelled into a roar in his rear. Yet
when we read the " Notes " we can find little offence
in them, and, to say truth, less interest than usual.
They are no true picture of America, or even of his
vision of America, and this for two reasons. First,
that he deliberately excluded from them all mention of that copyright question which had really
given him his glimpse of how tyrannical a democracy can he. Second, that here he chiefly criticizes
America for faults which are not, after all, especially American. For example, he is indignant with
the inadequate character of the prisons, and compares them unfavourably with those in England,
controlled by Lieutenant Tracey, and by Chesterton at Coldbath Fields, two reformers of prison

discipline for whom he had a high regard. But it was a mere accident that American gaols were inferior to English. There was and is nothing in the American spirit to prevent their effecting all the reforms of Tracey and Chesterton, nothing to prevent their doing anything that money and energy and organization can do. America might have (for all I know, does have) a prison system cleaner and more humane and more efficient than any other in the world. And the evil genius of America might still remain—everything might remain that makes Pogram or Chollop irritating or absurd. And against the evil genius of America Dickens was now to strike a second and a very different blow.

In January, 1843, appeared the first number of the novel called "Martin Chuzzlewit." The earlier part of the book and the end, which have no connection with America or the American problem, in any case require a passing word. But except for the two gigantic grotesques on each side of the gateway of the tale, Pecksniff and Mrs. Gamp, "Martin Chuzzlewit" will be chiefly admired for its American excursion. It is a good satire embedded in an indifferent novel. Mrs. Gamp is, indeed, a sumptuous study, laid on in those rich, oily, almost greasy colours that go to make the English comic characters, that make the very diction

of Falstaff fat, and quaking with jolly degradation. Pecksniff also is almost perfect, and much
too good to be true. The only other thing to be
noticed about him is that here, as almost everywhere else in the novels, the best figures are at
their best when they have least to do. Dickens's
characters are perfect as long as he can keep them
out of his stories. Bumble is divine until a dark
and practical secret is entrusted to him—as if anybody but a lunatic would entrust a secret to
Bumble. Micawber is noble when he is doing
nothing; but he is quite unconvincing when he is
spying on Uriah Heep, for obviously neither
Micawber nor any one else would employ Micawber
as a private detective. Similarly, while Pecksniff
is the best thing in the story, the story is the
worst thing in Pecksniff. His plot against old
Martin can only be described by saying that it is as
silly as old Martin's plot against him. His fall at
the end is one of the rare falls of Dickens. Surely
it was not necessary to take Pecksniff so seriously.
Pecksniff is a merely laughable character; he is
so laughable that he is lovable. Why take such
trouble to unmask a man whose mask you have
made transparent? Why collect all the characters
to witness the exposure of a man in whom none of
the characters believe? Why toil and triumph to

have the laugh of a man who was only made to be laughed at?

But it is the American part of "Martin Chuzzlewit" which is our concern, and which is memorable. It has the air of a great satire; but if it is only a great slander, it is still great. His serious book on America was merely a squib, perhaps a damp squib. In any case, we all know that America will survive such serious books. But his fantastic book may survive America. It may survive America as "The Knights" has survived Athens. "Martin Chuzzlewit" has this quality of great satire that the critic forgets to ask whether the portrait is true to the original, because the portrait is so much more important than the original. Who cares whether Aristophanes correctly describes Kleon, who is dead, when he so perfectly describes the demagogue, who cannot die? Just as little, it may be, will some future age care whether the ancient civilization of the west, the lost cities of New York and St. Louis, were fairly depicted in the colossal monument of Elijah Pogram. For there is much more in the American episodes than their intoxicating absurdity; there is more than humour in the young man who made the speech about the British Lion, and said, "I taunt that lion. Alone I dare him;" or in the

other man who told Martin that when he said
that Queen Victoria did not live in the Tower of
London he "fell into an error not uncommon
among his countrymen." He has his finger on the
nerve of an evil which was not only in his enemies,
but in himself. The great democrat has hold of
one of the dangers of democracy. The great optimist confronts a horrible nightmare of optimism.
Above all, the genuine Englishman attacks a sin
that is not merely American, but English also.
The eternal, complacent iteration of patriotic half-
truths; the perpetual buttering of one's self all
over with the same stale butter; above all, the big
defiances of small enemies, or the very urgent
challenges to very distant enemies; the cowardice
so habitual and unconscious that it wears the
plumes of courage—all this is an English temptation as well as an American one. "Martin Chuzzlewit" may be a caricature of America. America
may be a caricature of England. But in the gravest
college, in the quietest country house of England,
there is the seed of the same essential madness
that fills Dickens's book, like an asylum, with
brawling Chollops and raving Jefferson Bricks.
That essential madness is the idea that the good
patriot is the man who feels at ease about his
country. This notion of patriotism was unknown

in the little pagan republics where our European
patriotism began. It was unknown in the Middle
Ages. In the eighteenth century, in the making of
modern politics, a "patriot" meant a discontented
man. It was opposed to the word "courtier,"
which meant an upholder of present conditions. In
all other modern countries, especially in countries
like France and Ireland, where real difficulties have
been faced, the word "patriot" means something
like a political pessimist. This view and these
countries have exaggerations and dangers of their
own; but the exaggeration and danger of England
is the same as the exaggeration and danger of
The Water-Toast Gazette. The thing which is
rather foolishly called the Anglo-Saxon civilization
is at present soaked through with a weak pride.
It uses great masses of men not to procure discussion but to procure the pleasure of unanimity;
it uses masses like bolsters. It uses its organs
of public opinion not to warn the public, but to
soothe it. It really succeeds not only in ignoring
the rest of the world, but actually in forgetting it.
And when a civilization really forgets the rest of
the world—lets it fall as something obviously dim
and barbaric—then there is only one adjective
for the ultimate fate of that civilization, and that
adjective is "Chinese."

Martin Chuzzlewit's America is a mad-house: but it is a mad-house we are all on the road to. For completeness and even comfort are almost the definitions of insanity. The lunatic is the man who lives in a small world but thinks it is a large one: he is the man who lives in a tenth of the truth, and thinks it is the whole. The madman cannot conceive any cosmos outside a certain tale or conspiracy or vision. Hence the more clearly we see the world divided into Saxons and non-Saxons, into our splendid selves and the rest, the more certain we may be that we are slowly and quietly going mad. The more plain and satisfying our state appears, the more we may know that we are living in an unreal world. For the real world is not satisfying. The more clear become the colours and facts of Anglo-Saxon superiority, the more surely we may know we are in a dream. For the real world is not clear or plain. The real world is full of bracing bewilderments and brutal surprises. Comfort is the blessing and the curse of the English, and of Americans of the Pogram type also. With them it is a loud comfort, a wild comfort, a screaming and capering comfort; but comfort at bottom still. For there is but an inch of difference between the cushioned chamber and the padded cell.

CHAPTER VII

DICKENS AND CHRISTMAS

IN the July of 1844 Dickens went on an Italian
tour, which he afterwards summarized in the
book called " Pictures from Italy." They are, of
course, very vivacious, but there is no great need
to insist on them considered as Italian sketches ;
there is no need whatever to worry about them as
a phase of the mind of Dickens when he travelled
out of England. He never travelled out of England.
There is no trace in all these amusing pages that
he really felt the great foreign things which lie
in wait for us in the south of Europe, the Latin
civilization, the Catholic Church, the art of the
centre, the endless end of Rome. His travels are
not travels in Italy, but travels in Dickensland.
He sees amusing things ; he describes them amu-
singly. But he would have seen things just as
good in a street in Pimlico, and described them
just as well. Few things were racier even in his
raciest novel, than his description of the marionette
play of the death of Napoleon. Nothing could be
more perfect than the figure of the doctor, which

had something wrong with its wires, and hence
"hovered about the couch and delivered medical
opinions in the air." Nothing could be better as a
catching of the spirit of all popular drama than the
colossal depravity of the wooden image of "Sir
Uudson Low." But there is nothing Italian about
it. Dickens would have made just as good fun,
indeed just the same fun, of a Punch and Judy
show performing in Long Acre or Lincoln's Inn
Fields.

Dickens uttered just and sincere satire on
Plornish and Podsnap; but Dickens was as English
as any Podsnap or any Plornish. He had a hearty
humanitarianism, and a hearty sense of justice to
all nations, so far as he understood it. But that
very kind of humanitarianism, that very kind of
justice, were English. He was the Englishman of
the type that made Free Trade, the most English
of all things, since it was at once calculating and
optimistic. He respected catacombs and gondolas,
but that very respect was English. He wondered
at brigands and volcanoes, but that very wonder
was English. The very conception that Italy consists of these things was an English conception.
The root things he never understood, the Roman
legend, the ancient life of the Mediterranean, the
world-old civilization of the vine and olive, the

mystery of the immutable Church. He never understood these things, and I am glad he never understood them: he could only have understood them by ceasing to be the inspired cockney that he was, the rousing English Radical of the great Radical age in England. That spirit of his was one of the things that we have had which were truly national. All other forces we have borrowed, especially those which flatter us most. Imperialism is foreign, socialism is foreign, militarism is foreign, education is foreign, strictly even Liberalism is foreign. But Radicalism was our own; as English as the hedge-rows.

Dickens abroad, then, was for all serious purposes simply the Englishman abroad; the Englishman abroad is for all serious purposes, simply the Englishman at home. Of this generalization one modification must be made. Dickens did feel a direct pleasure in the bright and busy exterior of the French life, the clean caps, the coloured uniforms, the skies like blue enamel, the little green trees, the little white houses, the scene picked out in primary colours, like a child's picture-book. This he felt, and this he put (by a stroke of genius) into the mouth of Mrs. Lirriper, a London landlady on a holiday: for Dickens always knew that it is the simple and not the subtle who feel differences;

and he saw all his colours through the clear eyes
of the poor. And in thus taking to his heart the
streets, as it were, rather than the spires of the
Continent, he showed beyond question that combination of which we have spoken—of common sense
with uncommon sensibility. For it is for the sake
of the streets and shops and the coats and hats,
that we should go abroad ; they are far better worth
going to see than the castles and cathedrals and
Roman camps. For the wonders of the world are
the same all over the world, at least all over the
European world. Castles that throw valleys in
shadow, minsters that strike the sky, roads so old
that they seem to have been made by the gods,
these are in all Christian countries. The marvels
of man are at all our doors. A labourer hoeing
turnips in Sussex has no need to be ignorant that
the bones of Europe are the Roman roads. A clerk
living in Lambeth has no need not to know that
there was a Christian art exuberant in the thirteenth
century; for only across the river he can see the
live stones of the Middle Ages surging together
towards the stars. But exactly the things that do
strike the traveller as extraordinary are the ordinary
things, the food, the clothes, the vehicles ; the
strange things are cosmopolitan, the common things
are national and peculiar. Cologne spire is lifted

on the same arches as Canterbury ; but the thing
you cannot see out of Germany is a German beer-
garden.   There is no need for a Frenchman to go
to look at Westminster Abbey as a piece of English
architecture ; it is not in the special sense, a piece
of English architecture.   But a hansom cab is a
piece of English architecture ; a thing produced by
the peculiar poetry of our cities, a symbol of a
certain reckless comfort which is really English ;
a thing to draw a pilgrimage of the nations.   The
imaginative Englishman will be found all day in a
café; the imaginative Frenchman in a hansom cab.

This sort of pleasure Dickens took in the Latin
life ; but no deeper kind.   And the strongest of all
possible indications of his fundamental detachment
from it can be found in one fact.   A great part of
the time that he was in Italy he was engaged in
writing "The Chimes," and such Christmas tales,
tales of Christmas in the English towns, tales full
of fog and snow and hail and happiness.

Dickens could find in any street divergences
between man and man deeper than the divisions
of nations.   His fault was to exaggerate differences.
He could find types almost as distinct as separate
tribes of animals in his own brain and his own
city, those two homes of a magnificent chaos.   The
only two southerners introduced prominently into

his novels, the two in "Little Dorrit" are popular English foreigners, I had almost said stage foreigners. Villainy is, in English eyes, a southern trait, therefore one of the foreigners is villainous. Vivacity is, in English eyes, another southern trait, therefore the other foreigner is vivacious. But we can see from the outlines of both that Dickens did not have to go to Italy to get them. While poor panting millionaires, poor tired earls and poor God-forsaken American men of culture are plodding about Italy for literary inspiration, Charles Dickens made up the whole of that Italian romance (as I strongly suspect) from the faces of two London organ-grinders.

In the sunlight of the southern world, he was still dreaming of the firelight of the north. Among the palaces and the white campanili, he shut his eyes to see Marylebone and dreamed a lovely dream of chimney-pots. He was not happy he said, without streets. The very foulness and smoke of London were lovable in his eyes and fill his Christmas tales with a vivid vapour. In the clear skies of the south he saw afar off the fog of London like a sunset cloud and longed to be in the core of it.

This Christmas tone of Dickens, in connection with his travels, is a matter that can only be expressed by a parallel with one of his other works.

Much the same that has here been said of his
"Pictures from Italy," may be said about his "Child's
History of England;" with the difference that
while the "Pictures from Italy," do in a sense add
to his fame the "History of England" in almost
every sense detracts from it. But the nature of
the limitation is the same. What Dickens was
travelling in distant lands, that he was travelling
in distant ages; a sturdy, sentimental English
Radical with a large heart and a narrow mind.
He could not help falling into that besetting sin or
weakness of the modern progressive, the habit of
regarding the contemporary questions as the
eternal questions and the latest word as the last.
He could not get out of his head the instinctive
conception that the real problem before St. Dunstan
was whether he should support Lord John Russell
or Sir Robert Peel. He could not help seeing the
remotest peaks lit up by the raging bonfire of his
own passionate political crisis. He lived for the
instant and its urgency; that is, he did what St.
Dunstan did. He lived in an eternal present like
all simple men. It is indeed "A Child's History
of England;" but the child is the writer and not
the reader.

But Dickens in his cheapest cockney utilitarianism, was not only English, but unconsciously

historic. Upon him descended the real tradition
of "Merry England," and not upon the pallid
mediævalists who thought they were reviving it.
The Pre-Raphaelites, the Gothicists, the admirers of
the Middle Ages, had in their subtlety and sadness
the spirit of the present day. Dickens had in his
buffoonery and bravery the spirit of the Middle
Ages. He was much more mediæval in his attacks
on mediævalism than they were in their defences
of it. It was he who had the things of Chaucer,
the love of large jokes and long stories and brown
ale and all the white roads of England. Like
Chaucer he loved story within story, every man
telling a tale. Like Chaucer he saw something
openly comic in men's motley trades. Sam Weller
would have been a great gain to the Canterbury
Pilgrimage and told an admirable story. Rossetti's
Damozel would have been a great bore, regarded
as too fast by the Prioress and too priggish by
the Wife of Bath. It is said that in the somewhat
sickly Victorian revival of feudalism which was
called "Young England," a nobleman hired a
hermit to live in his grounds. It is also said that
the hermit struck for more beer. Whether this
ancedote be true or not, it is always told as showing a collapse from the ideal of the Middle Ages
to the level of the present day. But in the mere

act of striking for beer the holy man was very
much more "mediæval" than the fool who employed him.

It would be hard to find a better example of
this than Dickens's great defence of Christmas. In
fighting for Christmas he was fighting for the old
European festival, Pagan and Christian, for that
trinity of eating, drinking and praying which to
moderns appears irreverent, for the holy day
which is really a holiday. He had himself the
most babyish ideas about the past. He supposed
the Middle Ages to have consisted of tournaments
and torture-chambers, he supposed himself to be a
brisk man of the manufacturing age, almost a Utilitarian. But for all that he defended the mediæval
feast which was going out against the Utilitarianism
which was coming in. He could only see all that
was bad in mediævalism. But he fought for all
that was good in it. And he was all the more
really in sympathy with the old strength and
simplicity because he only knew that it was good
and did not know that it was old. He cared as
little for mediævalism as the mediævals did. He
cared as much as they did for lustiness and virile
laughter and sad tales of good lovers and pleasant
tales of good livers. He would have been very
much bored by Ruskin and Walter Pater if they

had explained to him the strange sunset tints of Lippi and Boticelli. He had no pleasure in looking on the dying Middle Ages. But he looked on the living Middle Ages, on a piece of the old uproarious superstition still unbroken; and he hailed it like a new religion. The Dickens character ate pudding to an extent at which the modern mediævalists turned pale. They would do every kind of honour to an old observance, except observing it. They would pay to a Church feast every sort of compliment except feasting.

And (as I have said) as were his unconscious relations to our European past, so were his unconscious relations to England. He imagined himself to be, if anything, a sort of cosmopolitan; at any rate to be a champion of the charms and merits of continental lands against the arrogance of our island. But he was in truth very much more a champion of the old and genuine England against that comparatively cosmopolitan England which we have all lived to see. And here again the supreme example is Christmas. Christmas is, as I have said, one of numberless old European feasts of which the essence is the combination of religion with merry-making. But among those feasts it is also especially and distinctively English in the style of its merry-making and even in the style of its religion. For the character of Christmas (as distinct, for instance, from the continental Easter) lies chiefly in two things; first on the terrestrial side the note of comfort rather than the note of brightness; and on the spiritual side, Christian charity rather than Christian ecstasy. And comfort is, like charity, a very English instinct. Nay, comfort is, like charity, an English merit; though our comfort may and does degenerate into materialism, just as our charity may and does degenerate into laxity and make-believe.

This ideal of comfort belongs peculiarly to England; it belongs peculiarly to Christmas; above all, it belongs pre-eminently to Dickens. And it is astonishingly misunderstood. It is misunderstood by the continent of Europe, it is, if possible, still more misunderstood by the English of to-day. On the Continent the restaurateurs provide us with raw beef, as if we were savages; yet old English cooking takes as much care as French. And in England has arisen a parvenu patriotism which represents the English as everything but English; as a blend of Chinese stoicism, Latin militarism, Prussian rigidity, and American bad taste. And so England, whose fault is gentility and whose virtue is geniality, England with her tradition of the great gay gentlemen of Elizabeth, is represented to the four quarters of the world (as in Mr. Kipling's religious poems) in the enormous image of a solemn cad. And because it is very difficult to be comfortable in the suburbs, the suburbs have voted that comfort is a gross and material thing. Comfort, especially this vision of Christmas comfort, is the reverse of a gross or material thing. It is far more poetical, properly speaking, than the Garden of Epicurus. It is far more artistic than the Palace of Art. It is more artistic because it is based upon a contrast, a contrast between the fire and wine within the house and the winter and the roaring rains without. It is far more poetical, because there is in it a note of defence, almost of war; a note of being besieged by the snow and hail; of making merry in the belly of a fort. The man who said that an Englishman's house is his castle said much more than he meant. The Englishman thinks of his house as something fortified, and provisioned, and his very surliness is at root romantic. And this sense would naturally be strongest in wild winter nights, when the lowered port-cullis and the lifted drawbridge do not merely bar people out, but bar people in. The Englishman's house is most sacred, not merely when the King cannot enter it, but when the Englishman cannot get out of it.

This comfort, then, is an abstract thing, a

principle.   The English poor shut all their doors
and windows till their rooms reek like the Black
Hole.   They are suffering for an idea.   Mere animal
hedonism would not dream, as we English do, of
winter feasts and little rooms, but of eating fruit in
large and idle gardens.   Mere sensuality would
desire to please all its senses.   But to our good
dreams this dark and dangerous background is
essential; the highest pleasure we can imagine is a
defiant pleasure, a happiness that stands at bay.
The word " comfort " is not indeed the right word,
it conveys too much of the slander of mere sense ;
the true word is " cosiness," a word not translat-
able.   One, at least, of the essentials of it is smallness, smallness in preference to largeness, smallness
for smallness' sake.   The merry-maker wants a
pleasant parlour, he would not give twopence
for a pleasant continent.   In our difficult time, of
course, a fight for mere space has become necessary.
Instead of being greedy for ale and Christmas
pudding we are greedy for mere air, an equally
sensual appetite.   In abnormal conditions this is
wise ; and the illimitable veldt is an excellent thing
for nervous people.   But our fathers were large
and healthy enough to make a thing humane, and
not worry about whether it was hygienic.   They
were big enough to get into small rooms.

Of this quite deliberate and artistic quality in the close Christmas chamber, the standing evidence is Dickens in Italy. He created these dim firelit tales like little dim red jewels, as an artistic necessity, in the centre of an endless summer. Amid the white cities of Tuscany he hungered for something romantic, and wrote about a rainy Christmas. Amid the pictures of the Uffizi he starved for something beautiful, and fed his memory on London fog. His feeling for the fog was especially poignant and typical. In the first of his Christmas tales, the popular "Christmas Carol," he suggested the very soul of it in one simile, when he spoke of the dense air, suggesting that "Nature was brewing on a large scale." This sense of the thick atmosphere as something to eat or drink, something not only solid but satisfactory, may seem almost insane, but it is no exaggeration of Dickens's emotion. We speak of a fog "that you could cut with a knife." Dickens would have liked the phrase as suggesting that the fog was a colossal cake. He liked even more his own phrase of the Titanic brewery, and no dream would have given him a wilder pleasure than to grope his way to some such tremendous vats and drink the ale of the giants.

There is a current prejudice against fogs, and Dickens, perhaps, is their only poet. Considered hygienically, no doubt this may be more or less excusable. But, considered poetically, fog is not undeserving, it has a real significance. We have in our great cities abolished the clean and sane darkness of the country. We have outlawed night and sent her wandering in wild meadows; we have lit eternal watch-fires against her return. We have made a new cosmos, and as a consequence our own sun and stars. And as a consequence also, and most justly, we have made our own darkness. Just as every lamp is a warm human moon, so every fog is a rich human nightfall. If it were not for this mystic accident we should never see darkness, and he who has never seen darkness has never seen the sun. Fog for us is the chief form of that outward pressure which compresses mere luxury into real comfort. It makes the world small, in the same spirit as in that common and happy cry that the world is small, meaning that it is full of friends. The first man that emerges out of the mist with a light, is for us Prometheus, a saviour bringing fire to men. He is that greatest and best of all men, greater than the heroes, better than the saints, Man Friday. Every rumble of a cart, every cry in the distance, marks the heart of humanity beating undaunted in the darkness. It is wholly human ; man toiling in his own cloud. If real darkness is

like the embrace of God, this is the dark embrace
of man.

In such a sacred cloud the tale called "The
Christmas Carol" begins, the first and most typical
of all his Christmas tales. It is not irrelevant to
dilate upon the geniality of this darkness, because
it is characteristic of Dickens that his atmospheres
are more important than his stories. The Christmas atmosphere is more important than Scrooge,
or the ghosts either ; in a sense, the background
is more important than the figures. The same
thing may be noticed in his dealings with that
other atmosphere (besides that of good humour),
which he excelled in creating, an atmosphere of
mystery and wrong, such as that which gathers
round Mrs. Clennam, rigid in her chair, or old
Miss Havisham, ironically robed as a bride. Here
again the atmosphere altogether eclipses the story,
which often seems disappointing in comparison.
The secrecy is sensational ; the secret is tame.
The surface of the thing seems more awful than the
core of it. It seems almost as if these grisly
figures, Mrs. Chadband and Mrs. Clennam, Miss
Havisham and Miss Flite, Nemo and Sally Brass,
were keeping something back from the author as
well as from the reader. When the book closes we
do not know their real secret. They soothed the

optimistic Dickens with something less terrible
than the truth. The dark house of Arthur Clennam's childhood really depresses us; it is a true
glimpse into that quiet street in hell, where live
the children of that unique dispensation which
theologians call Calvinism and Christians devil-
worship. But some stranger crime had really been
done there, some more monstrous blasphemy or
human sacrifice than the suppression of some silly
document advantageous to the silly Dorrits. Something worse than a common tale of jilting lay
behind the masquerade and madness of the awful
Miss Havisham. Something worse was whispered
by the misshapen Quilp to the sinister Sally in
that wild, wet summer-house by the river, something worse than the clumsy plot against the
clumsy Kit. These dark pictures seem almost as
if they were literally visions; things, that is, that
Dickens saw but did not understand.

And as with his backgrounds of gloom, so with
his backgrounds of good-will, in such tales as
"The Christmas Carol." The tone of the tale is
kept throughout in a happy monotony, though the
tale is everywhere irregular and in some places
weak. It has the same kind of artistic unity that
belongs to a dream. A dream may begin with the
end of the world and end with a tea-party; but

either the end of the world will seem as trivial
as a tea-party or that tea-party will be as terrible
as the day of doom.   The incidents change wildly ;
the story scarcely changes at all.   "The Christmas
Carol" is a kind of philanthropic dream, an enjoyable nightmare, in which the scenes shift bewilder-
ingly and seem as miscellaneous as the pictures in
a scrap-book, but in which there is one constant
state of the soul, a state of rowdy benediction and
a hunger for human faces.   The beginning is about
a winter day and a miser ; yet the beginning is in
no way bleak.   The author starts with a kind of
happy howl ; he bangs on our door like a drunken
carol singer ; his style is festive and popular ; he
compares the snow and hail to philanthropists who
"come down handsomely" ; he compares the fog
to unlimited beer.   Scrooge is not really inhuman
at the beginning any more than he is at the end.
There is a heartiness in his inhospitable sentiments
that is akin to humour and therefore to humanity ;
he is only a crusty old bachelor, and had (I strongly
suspect) given away turkeys secretly all his life.
The beauty and the real blessing of the story do
not lie in the mechanical plot of it, the repentance
of Scrooge, probable or improbable ; they lie in
the great furnace of real happiness that glows
through Scrooge and everything round him ; that

great furnace, the heart of Dickens. Whether the
Christmas visions would or would not convert
Scrooge, they convert us. Whether or no the
visions were evoked by real Spirits of the Past,
Present, and Future, they were evoked by that
truly exalted order of angels who are correctly
called High Spirits. They are impelled and sustained by a quality which our contemporary artists
ignore or almost deny, but which in a life decently
lived is as normal and attainable as sleep, positive,
passionate, conscious joy. The story sings from
end to end like a happy man going home ; and, like
a happy and good man, when it cannot sing it yells.
It is lyric and exclamatory, from the first exclamatory words of it. It is strictly a Christmas Carol.

Dickens, as has been said, went to Italy with
this kindly cloud still about him, still meditating
on Yule mysteries. Among the olives and the
orange-trees he wrote his second great Christmas
tale, "The Chimes," at Genoa in 1844, a Christmas
tale only differing from "The Christmas Carol" in
being fuller of the grey rains of winter and the
north. "The Chimes" is, like the "Carol," an
appeal for charity and mirth, but it is a stern and
fighting appeal : if the other is a Christmas carol,
this is a Christmas war-song. In it Dickens hurled
himself with even more than his usual militant joy

and scorn into an attack upon a cant, which he said
made his blood boil. This cant was nothing more
nor less than the whole tone taken by three-quarters
of the political and economic world towards the
poor. It was a vague and vulgar Benthamism with
a rollicking Tory touch in it. It explained to the
poor their duties with a cold and coarse philanthropy unendurable by any free man. It had also
at its command a kind of brutal banter, a loud good
humour which Dickens sketches savagely in Alder-
man Cute. He fell furiously on all their ideas : the
cheap advice to live cheaply, the base advice to
live basely, above all, the preposterous primary
assumption that the rich are to advise the poor
and not the poor the rich. There were and are
hundreds of these benevolent bullies. Some say
that the poor should give up having children,
which means that they should give up their great
virtue of sexual sanity. Some say that they should
give up " treating " each other, which means that
they should give up all that remains to them of
the virtue of hospitality. Against all of this
Dickens thundered very thoroughly in "The
Chimes." It may be remarked in passing that
this affords another instance of a confusion already
referred to, the confusion whereby Dickens supposed himself to be exalting the present over the

past, whereas he was really dealing deadly blows at things strictly peculiar to the present. Embedded in this very book is a somewhat useless interview between Trotty Veck and the church bells, in which the latter lecture the former for having supposed (why, I don't know) that they were expressing regret for the disappearance of the Middle Ages. There is no reason why Trotty Veck or any one else should idealize the Middle Ages, but certainly he was the last man in the world to be asked to idealize the nineteenth century, seeing that the smug and stingy philosophy, which poisons his life through the book, was an exclusive creation of that century. But, as I have said before, the fieriest mediævalist may forgive Dickens for disliking the good things the Middle Ages took away, considering how he loved whatever good things the Middle Ages left behind. It matters very little that he hated old feudal castles when they were already old. It matters very much that he hated the New Poor Law while it was still new.

The moral of this matter in "The Chimes" is essential. Dickens had sympathy with the poor in the Greek and literal sense; he suffered with them mentally; for the things that irritated them were the things that irritated him. He did not

pity the people, or even champion the people, or
even merely love the people; in this matter he
was the people. He alone in our literature is the
voice not merely of the social substratum, but even
of the subconsciousness of the substratum.   He
utters the secret anger of the humble. He says
what the uneducated only think, or even only feel,
about the educated.   And in nothing is he so
genuinely such a voice as in this fact of his fiercest
mood being reserved for methods that are counted
scientific and progressive.   Pure and exalted
atheists talk themselves into believing that the
working-classes are turning with indignant scorn
from the churches. The working-classes are not
indignant against the churches in the least. The
things the working-classes really are indignant
against are the hospitals. The people has no
definite disbelief in the temples of theology. The
people has a very fiery and practical disbelief in
the temples of physical science. The things the
poor hate are the modern things, the rationalistic
things—doctors, inspectors, poor law guardians,
professional philanthropy.   They never showed
any reluctance to be helped by the old and corrupt
monasteries. They will often die rather than be
helped by the modern and efficient workhouse.
Of all this anger, good or bad, Dickens is the voice

of an accusing energy. When, in " The Christmas
Carol," Scrooge refers to the surplus population,
the Spirit tells him, very justly, not to speak till
he knows what the surplus is and where it is.
The implication is severe but sound. When a
group of superciliously benevolent economists
look down into the abyss for the surplus population, assuredly there is only one answer that
should be given to them; and that is to say, "If
there is a surplus, you are a surplus." And if any
one were ever cut off, they would be. If the barri-
cades went up in our streets and the poor became
masters, I think the priests would escape, I fear
the gentlemen would ; but I believe the gutters
would be simply running with the blood of
philanthropists.

Lastly, he was at one with the poor in this
chief matter of Christmas, in the matter, that is,
of special festivity. There is nothing on which
the poor are more criticized than on the point of
spending large sums on small feasts; and though
there are material difficulties, there is nothing in
which they are more right. It is said that a Boston
paradox-monger said, "Give us the luxuries of life
and we will dispense with the necessities." But it
is the whole human race that says it, from the first
savage wearing feathers instead of clothes to the

last costermonger having a treat instead of three meals.

The third of his Christmas stories, "The Cricket on the Hearth," calls for no extensive comment, though it is very characteristic. It has all the qualities which we have called dominant qualities in his Christmas sentiment. It has cosiness, that is the comfort that depends upon a discomfort surrounding it. It has a sympathy with the poor, and especially with the extravagance of the poor; with what may be called the temporary wealth of the poor. It has the sentiment of the hearth, that is, the sentiment of the open fire being the red heart of the room. That open fire is the veritable flame of England, still kept burning in the midst of a mean civilization of stoves. But everything that is valuable in "The Cricket on the Hearth" is perhaps as well expressed in the title as it is in the story. The tale itself, in spite of some of those inimitable things that Dickens never failed to say, is a little too comfortable to be quite convincing. "The Christmas Carol" is the conversion of an anti-Christmas character. "The Chimes" is a slaughter of anti-Christmas characters. "The Cricket," perhaps, fails for lack of this crusading note. For everything has its weak side, and when full justice has been done to this neglected note of poetic comfort, we must remember that it has its very real weak side. The defect of it in the work of Dickens was that he tended sometimes to pile up the cushions until none of the characters could move. He is so much interested in effecting his state of static happiness that he forgets to make a story at all. His princes at the start of the story begin to live happily ever afterwards. We feel this strongly in "Master Humphrey's Clock," and we feel it sometimes in these Christmas stories. He makes his characters so comfortable that his characters begin to dream and drivel. And he makes his reader so comfortable that his reader goes to sleep.

The actual tale of the carrier and his wife sounds somewhat sleepily in our ears ; we cannot keep our attention fixed on it, though we are conscious of a kind of warmth from it as from a great wood fire. We know so well that everything will soon be all right that we do not suspect when the carrier suspects, and are not frightened when the gruff Tackleton growls. The sound of the Christmas festivities at the end come fainter on our ears than did the shout of the Cratchits or the bells of Trotty Veck. All the good figures that followed Scrooge when he came growling out of the fog fade into the fog again.

CHAPTER VIII

THE TIME OF TRANSITION

DICKENS was back in London by the June of 1845. About this time he became the first editor of *The Daily News*, a paper which he had largely planned and suggested, and which, I trust, remembers its semi-divine origin. That his thoughts had been running, as suggested in the last chapter, somewhat monotonously on his Christmas domesticities, is again suggested by the rather singular fact that he originally wished *The Daily News* to be called *The Cricket*. Probably he was haunted again with his old vision of a homely, tale-telling periodical such as had broken off in "Master Humphrey's Clock." About this time, however, he was peculiarly unsettled. Almost as soon as he had taken the editorship he threw it up; and having only recently come back to England, he soon made up his mind to go back to the Continent. In the May of 1846 he ran over to Switzerland and tried to write "Dombey and Son" at Lausanne. Tried to, I say, because his letters are full of an angry impotence. He could

not get on. He attributed this especially to his
love of London and his loss of it, "the absence of
streets and numbers of figures. . . . *My* figures
seem disposed to stagnate without crowds about
them." But he also, with shrewdness, attributed
it more generally to the laxer and more wandering
life he had led for the last two years, the American
tour, the Italian tour, diversified, generally speaking, only with slight literary productions. His
ways were never punctual or healthy, but they
were also never unconscientious as far as work
was concerned. If he walked all night he could
write all day. But in this strange exile or inter-
regnum he did not seem able to fall into any habits,
even bad habits. A restlessness beyond all his
experience had fallen for a season upon the most
restless of the children of men.

It may be a mere coincidence : but this break in
his life very nearly coincided with the important
break in his art. "Dombey and Son," planned in
all probability some time before, was destined to
be the last of a quite definite series, the early novels
of Dickens. The difference between the books
from the beginning up to "Dombey," and the
books from "David Copperfield" to the end may
be hard to state dogmatically, but is evident to
every one with any literary sense. Very coarsely,

the case may be put by saying that he diminished, in the story as a whole, the practice of pure caricature. Still more coarsely it may be put in the phrase that he began to practise realism. If we take Mr. Stiggins, say, as a clergyman depicted at the beginning of his literary career, and Mr. Crisparkle, say, as a clergyman depicted at the end of it, it is evident that the difference does not merely consist in the fact that the first is a less desirable clergyman than the second. It consists in the nature of our desire for either of them. The glory of Mr. Crisparkle partly consists in the fact that he might really exist anywhere, in any country town into which we may happen to stray. The glory of Mr. Stiggins wholly consists in the fact that he could not possibly exist anywhere except in the head of Dickens. Dickens has the secret recipe of that divine dish. In some sense, therefore, when we say that he became less of a caricaturist we mean that he became less of a creator. That original violent vision of all things which he had seen from his boyhood began to be mixed with other men's milder visions and with the light of common day. He began to understand and practise other than his own mad merits ; began to have some movement towards the merits of other writers, towards the mixed emotion of Thackeray, or the solidity of George Eliot. And this must be said for the process; that the fierce wine of Dickens could endure some dilution. On the whole, perhaps, his primal personalism was all the better when surging against some saner restraints. Perhaps a flavour of strong Stiggins goes a long way. Perhaps the colossal Crummles might be cut down into six or seven quite credible characters. For my own part, for reasons which I shall afterwards mention, I am in real doubt about the advantage of this realistic education of Dickens. I am not sure that it made his books better; but I am sure it made them less bad. He made fewer mistakes undoubtedly; ·he succeeded] in eliminating much of the mere rant or cant of his first books; he threw away much of the old padding, all the more annoying, perhaps, in a literary sense, because he did not mean it for padding, but for essential eloquence. But he did not produce anything actually better than Mr. Chuckster. But then there is nothing better than Mr. Chuckster. Certain works of art, such as the Venus of Milo, exhaust our aspiration. Upon the whole this may, perhaps, be safely said of the transition. Those who have any doubt about Dickens can have no doubt of the superiority of the later books. Beyond question they have less of what annoys us in Dickens. But do not, if you are in the company of any ardent adorers of Dickens (as I hope for your sake you are) do not insist too urgently and exclusively on the splendour of Dickens's last works, or they will discover that you do not like him.

"Dombey and Son" is the last novel in the first manner: "David Copperfield" is the first novel in the last. The increase in care and realism in the second of the two is almost startling. Yet even in "Dombey and Son" we can see the coming of a change, however faint, if we compare it with his first fantasies such as "Nicholas Nickleby" or "The Old Curiosity Shop." The central story is still melodrama, but it is much more tactful and effective melodrama. Melodrama is a form of art, legitimate like any other, as noble as farce, almost as noble as pantomime. The essence of melodrama is that it appeals to the moral sense in a highly simplified state, just as farce appeals to the sense of humour in a highly simplified state. Farce creates people who are so intellectually simple as to hide in packing-cases or pretend to be their own aunts. Melodrama creates people so morally simple as to kill their enemies in Oxford Street, and repent on seeing their mother's photograph. The object of the simplification in farce and melodrama is the same, and quite artistically legitimate,

the object of gaining a resounding rapidity of
action which subtleties would obstruct. And this
can be done well or ill. The simplified villain can
be a spirited charcoal sketch or a mere black
smudge. Carker is a spirited charcoal sketch:
Ralph Nickleby is a mere black smudge. The
tragedy of Edith Dombey teems with unlikelihood,
but it teems with life. That Dombey should give
his own wife censure through his own business
manager is impossible, I will not say in a gentleman, but in a person of ordinary sane self-conceit.
But once having got the inconceivable trio before
the footlights, Dickens gives us good ringing
dialogue, very different from the mere rants in
which Ralph Nickleby figures in the unimaginable
character of a rhetorical money-lender. And there
is another point of technical improvement in this
book over such books as "Nicholas Nickleby."
It has not only a basic idea, but a good basic idea.
There is a real artistic opportunity in the conception of a solemn and selfish man of affairs, feeling
for his male heir, his first and last emotion, mingled
of a thin flame of tenderness and a strong flame of
pride. But with all these possibilities, the serious
episode of the Dombeys serves ultimately only to
show how unfitted Dickens was for such things,
how fitted he was for something opposite.

The incurable poetic character, the hopelessly non-realistic character of Dickens's essential genius could not have a better example than the story of the Dombeys. For the story itself is probable; it is the treatment that makes it unreal. In attempting to paint the dark pagan devotion of the father (as distinct from the ecstatic and Christian devotion of the mother) Dickens was painting something that was really there. This is no wild theme, like the wanderings of Nell's grandfather, or the marriage of Gride. A man of Dombey's type would love his son as he loves Paul. He would neglect his daughter as he neglects Florence. And yet we feel the utter unreality of it all, while we fell the utter reality of monsters like Stiggins or Mantalini. Dickens could only work in his own way, and that way was the wild way. We may almost say this: that he could only make his characters probable if he was allowed to make them impossible. Give him licence to say and do anything, and he could create beings as vivid as our own aunts and uncles. Keep him to likelihood and he could not tell the plainest tale so as to make it seem likely. The story of "Pickwick" is credible, although it is not possible. The story of Florence Dombey is incredible although it is true.

An excellent example can be found in the same

story.   Major Bagstock is a grotesque, and yet he
contains touch after touch of Dickens's quiet and
sane observation of things as they are.   He was
always most accurate when he was most fantastic.
Dombey and Florence are perfectly reasonable, but
we simply know that they do not exist.   The Major
is mountainously exaggerated, but we all feel that
we have met him at Brighton.   Nor is the rationale
of the paradox difficult to see ; Dickens exaggerated
when he had found a real truth to exaggerate.   It
is a deadly error (an error at the back of much of
the false placidity of our politics) to suppose that
lies are told with excess and luxuriance, and truths
told with modesty and restraint.   Some of the
most frantic lies on the face of life are told with
modesty and restraint; for the simple reason that
only modesty and restraint will save them.   Many
official declarations are just as dignified as Mr.
Dombey, because they are just as fictitious.   On
the other hand, the man who has found a truth
dances about like a boy who has found a shilling ;
he breaks into extravagances, as the Christian
churches broke into gargoyles.   In one sense truth
alone can be exaggerated ; nothing else can stand
the strain.   The outrageous Bagstock is a glowing
and glaring exaggeration of a thing we have all
seen in life—the worst and most dangerous of all

its hypocrisies.   For the worst and most dangerous
hypocrite is not he who affects unpopular virtue,
but he who affects popular vice.   The jolly fellow
of the saloon bar and the racecourse is the real
deceiver of mankind; he has misled more than any
false prophet, and his victims cry to him out of
hell.   The excellence of the Bagstock conception
can best be seen if we compare it with the much
weaker and more improbable knavery of Pecksniff.
It would not be worth a man's while, with any
worldly object, to pretend to be a holy and high-
minded architect.   The world does not admire holy
and high-minded architects.   The world does admire rough and tough old army men who swear at
waiters and wink at women.   Major Bagstock is
simply the perfect prophecy of that decadent
jingoism which corrupted England of late years.
England has been duped, not by the cant of goodness, but by the cant of badness.   It has been
fascinated by a quite fictitious cynicism, and
reached that last and strangest of all impostures
in which the mask is as repulsive as the face.

"Dombey and Son" provides us with yet
another instance of this general fact in Dickens.
He could only get to the most solemn emotions
adequately if he got to them through the grotesque.
He could only, so to speak, really get into the

inner chamber by coming down the chimney, like his own most lovable lunatic in "Nicholas Nickleby." A good example is such a character as Toots. Toots is what none of Dickens's dignified characters are, in the most serious sense, a true lover. He is the twin of Romeo. He has passion, humility, self-knowledge, a mind lifted into all magnanimous thoughts, everything that goes with the best kind of romantic love. His excellence in the art of love can only be expressed by the somewhat violent expression that he is as good a lover as Walter Gay is a bad one. Florence surely deserved her father's scorn if she could prefer Gay to Toots. It is neither a joke nor any kind of exaggeration to say that in the vacillations of Toots, Dickens not only came nearer to the psychology of true love than he ever came elsewhere, but nearer than any one else ever came. To ask for the loved one, and then not to dare to cross the threshhold, to be invited by her, to long to accept, and then to lie in order to decline, these are the funny things that Mr. Toots did, and that every honest man who yells with laughter at him has done also. For the moment, however, I only mention this matter as a pendant case to the case of Major Bagstock, an example of the way in which Dickens had to be ridiculous in order to begin to

be true. His characters that begin solemn end
futile; his characters that begin frivolous end
solemn in the best sense. His foolish figures are
not only more entertaining than his serious figures,
they are also much more serious. The Marchioness
is not only much more laughable than Little Nell;
she is also much more of all that Little Nell was
meant to be; much more really devoted, pathetic,
and brave. Dick Swiveller is not only a much
funnier fellow than Kit, he is also a much more
genuine fellow, being free from that slight stain of
"meekness," or the snobbishness of the respectable
poor, which the wise and perfect Chuckster wisely
and perfectly perceived in Kit. Susan Nipper is
not only more of a comic character than Florence;
she is more of a heroine than Florence any day of
the week. In "Our Mutual Friend" we do not, for
some reason or other, feel really very much excited
about the fall or rescue of Lizzie Hexam. She
seems too romantic to be really pathetic. But we
do feel excited about the rescue of Miss Lammle,
because she is, like Toots, a holy fool; because her
pink nose and pink elbows, and candid outcry and
open indecent affections do convey to us a sense
of innocence helpless among human dragons, of
Andromeda tied naked to a rock. Dickens had to
make a character humorous before he could make

it human; it was the only way he knew, and he ought to have always adhered to it. Whether he knew it or not, the only two really touching figures in " Martin Chuzzlewit " are the Misses Pecksniff. Of the things he tried to treat unsmilingly and grandly we can all make game to our heart's content. But when once he has laughed at a thing it is sacred for ever.

"Dombey," however, means first and foremost the finale of the early Dickens. It is difficult to say exactly in what it is that we perceive that the old crudity ends here, and does not reappear in " David Copperfield " or in any of the novels after it. But so certainly it is. In detached scenes and characters, indeed, Dickens kept up his farcical note almost or quite to the end. But this is the last farce; this is the last work in which a farcical licence is tacitly claimed, a farcical note struck to start with. And in a sense his next novel may be called his first novel. But the growth of this great novel, " David Copperfield," is a thing very interesting, but at the same time very dark, for it is a growth in the soul. We have seen that Dickens's mind was in a stir of change; that he was dreaming of art, and even of realism. Hugely delighted as he invariably was with his own books, he was humble enough to be ambitious. He was even

humble enough to be envious.   In the matter of
art, for instance, in the narrower sense, of arrangement and proportion in fictitious things, he began
to be conscious of his deficiency, and even, in a
stormy sort of way, ashamed of it; he tried to gain
completeness even while raging at any one who
called him incomplete.   And in this matter of
artistic construction, his ambition (and his success
too) grew steadily up to the instant of his death.
The end finds him attempting things that are at
the opposite pole to the frank formlessness of
"Pickwick."   His last book, "The Mystery of Edwin
Drood," depends entirely upon construction, even
upon a centralized strategy.   He staked everything
upon a plot; he who had been the weakest of
plotters, weaker than Sim Tappertit.   He essayed
a detective story, he who could never keep a
secret; and he has kept it to this day.   A new
Dickens was really being born when Dickens
died.

And as with art, so with reality.   He wished to
show that he could construct as well as anybody.
He also wished to show that he could be as
accurate as anybody.   And in this connection (as
in many others) we must recur constantly to the
facts mentioned in connection with America and
with his money-matters.   We must recur, I mean,

to the central fact that his desires were extravagant in quantity, but not in quality; that his wishes were excessive, but not eccentric. It must never be forgotten that sanity was his ideal, even when he seemed almost insane. It was thus with his literary aspirations. He was brilliant; but he wished sincerely to be solid. Nobody out of an asylum could deny that he was a genius and an unique writer; but he did not wish to be an unique writer, but an universal writer. Much of the manufactured pathos or rhetoric against which his enemies quite rightly rail, is really due to his desire to give all sides of life at once, to make his book a cosmos instead of a tale. He was sometimes really vulgar in his wish to be a literary Whiteley, an universal provider. Thus it was that he felt about realism and truth to life. Nothing is easier than to defend Dickens as Dickens, but Dickens wished to be everybody else. Nothing is easier than to defend Dickens's world as a fairyland, of which he alone has the key; to defend him as one defends Maeterlinck, or any other original writer. But Dickens was not content with being original, he had a wild wish to be true. He loved truth so much in the abstract that he sacrificed to the shadow of it his own glory. He denied his own divine originality, and pretended that he had plagiarized from life.

He disowned his own soul's children, and said he
had picked them up in the street.

And in this mixed and heated mood of anger
and ambition, vanity and doubt, a new and great
design was born. He loved to be romantic, yet he
desired to be real. How if he wrote of a thing
that was real and showed that it was romantic ?
He loved real life ; but he also loved his own way.
How if he wrote his own real life, but wrote it in
his own way ? How if he showed the carping
critics who doubted the existence of his strange
characters, his own yet stranger existence ? How
if he forced these pedants and unbelievers to admit
that Weller and Pecksniff, Crummles and Swiveller,
whom they thought so improbably wild and
wonderful, were less wild and wonderful than
Charles Dickens ? What if he ended the quarrels
about whether his romances could occur, by con-
fessing that his romance had occurred ?

For some time past, probably during the greater
part of his life, he had made notes for an autobiography. I have already quoted an admirable
passage from these notes, a passage reproduced
in " David Copperfield," with little more alteration
than a change of proper names—the passage which
describes Captain Porter and the debtor's petition
in the Marshalsea. But he probably perceived at

last what a less keen intelligence must ultimately have perceived, that if an autobiography is really to be honest it must be turned into a work of fiction. If it is really to tell the truth, it must at all costs profess not to. No man dare say of himself, over his own name, how badly he has behaved. No man dare say of himself, over his own name, how well he has behaved. Moreover, of course a touch of fiction is almost always essential to the real conveying of fact, because fact, as experienced, has a fragmentariness which is bewildering at first hand and quite blinding at second hand. Facts have at least to be sorted into compartments and the proper head and tail given back to each. The perfection and pointedness of art are a sort of substitute for the pungency of actuality. Without this selection and completion our life seems a tangle of unfinished tales, a heap of novels, all volume one. Dickens determined to make one complete novel of it.

For though there are many other aspects of "David Copperfield," this autobiographical aspect is, after all, the greatest. The point of the book is that, unlike all the other books of Dickens, it is concerned with quite common actualities, but it is concerned with them warmly and with the war-like sympathies. It is not only both realistic and romantic; it is realistic because it is romantic. It is human nature described with the human exaggeration. We all know the actual types in the book; they are not like the turgid and preternatural types elsewhere in Dickens. They are not purely poetic creations like Mr. Kenwigs or Mr. Bunsby. We all know that they exist. We all know the stiff-necked and humorous old-fashioned nurse, so conventional and yet so original, so dependent and yet so independent. We all know the intrusive step-father, the abstract strange male, coarse, handsome, sulky, successful, a breaker-up of homes. We all know the erect and sardonic spinster, the spinster who is so mad in small things and so sane in great ones. We all know the cock of the school; we all know Steerforth, the creature whom the gods love and even the servants respect. We know his poor and aristocratic mother, so proud, so gratified, so desolate. We know the Rosa Dartle type, the lonely woman in whom affection itself has stagnated into a sort of poison.

But while these are real characters they are real characters lit up with the colours of youth and passion. They are real people romantically felt; that is to say, they are real people felt as real people feel them. They are exaggerated, like all Dickens's figures: but they are not exaggerated

as personalities are exaggerated by an artist; they
are exaggerated as personalities are exaggerated
by their own friends and enemies. The strong
souls are seen through the glorious haze of the
emotions that strong souls really create. We have
Murdstone as he would be to a boy who hated
him; and rightly, for a boy would hate him. We
have Steerforth as he would be to a boy who
adored him; and rightly, for a boy would adore
him. It may be that if these persons had a mere
terrestrial existence, they appeared to other eyes
more insignificant. It may be that Murdstone in
common life was only a heavy business man with
a human side that David was too sulky to find.
It may be that Steerforth was only an inch or
two taller than David, and only a shade or two
above him in the lower middle classes; but this
does not make the book less true. In cataloguing
the facts of life the author must not omit that
massive fact, illusion.

When we say the book is true to life we must
stipulate that it is especially true to youth : even
to boyhood. All the characters seem a little larger
than they really were, for David is looking up at
them. And the early pages of the book are in
particular astonishingly vivid. Parts of it seem
like fragments of our forgotten infancy. The dark

house of childhood, the loneliness, the things half
understood, the nurse with her inscrutable sulks
and her more inscrutable tenderness, the sudden
deportations to distant places, the seaside and its
childish friendships, all this stirs in us when we
read it, like something out of a previous existence.
Above all, Dickens has excellently depicted the
child enthroned in that humble circle which only
in after years he perceives to have been humble.
Modern and cultured persons, I believe, object to
their children seeing kitchen company or being
taught by a woman like Peggotty. But surely it
is more important to be educated in a sense of
human dignity and equality than in anything else
in the world. And a child who has once had to
respect a kind and capable woman of the lower
classes will respect the lower classes for ever.
The true way to overcome the evil in class distinctions is not to denounce them as revolutionists
denounce them, but to ignore them as children
ignore them.

The early youth of David Copperfield is psycho-
logically almost as good as his childhood. In one
touch especially Dickens pierced the very core of
the sensibility of boyhood; it was when he made
David more afraid of a manservant than of anybody
or anything else. The lowering Murdstone, the

awful Mrs. Steerforth are not so alarming to him as Mr. Littimer, the unimpeachable gentleman's gentleman. This is exquisitely true to the masculine emotions, especially in their undeveloped state. A youth of common courage does not fear anything violent, but he is in mortal fear of anything correct. This may or may not be the reason that so few female writers understand their male characters, but this fact remains: that the more sincere and passionate and even headlong a lad is the more certain he is to be conventional. The bolder and freer he seems the more the traditions of the college or the rules of the club will hold him with their gyves of gossamer; and the less afraid he is of his enemies the more cravenly he will be afraid of his friends. Herein lies indeed the darkest peril of our ethical doubt and chaos. The fear is that as morals become less urgent, manners will become more so; and men who have forgotten the fear of God will retain the fear of Littimer. We shall merely sink into a much meaner bondage. For when you break the great laws, you do not get liberty; you do not even get anarchy. You get the small laws.

The sting and strength of this piece of fiction, then, do (by a rare accident) lie in the circumstance that it was so largely founded on fact. "David

Copperfield" is the great answer of a great romancer to the realists. David says in effect: "What! you say that the Dickens tales are too purple really to have happened! Why, this is what happened to me, and it seemed the most purple of all. You say that the Dickens heroes are too handsome and triumphant! Why, no prince or paladin in Ariosto was ever so handsome and triumphant as the Head Boy seemed to me walking before me in the sun. You say the Dickens villains are too black! Why, there was no ink in the devil's ink-stand black enough for my own step-father when I had to live in the same house with him. The facts are quite the other way to what you suppose. This life of grey studies and half tones, the absence of which you regret in Dickens, is only life as it is looked at. This life of heroes and villains is life as it is lived. The life a man knows best is exactly the life he finds most full of fierce certainties and battles between good and ill—his own. Oh yes, the life we do not care about may easily be a psychological comedy. Other people's lives may easily be human documents. But a man's own life is always a melodrama."

There are other effective things in "David Copperfield;" they are not all autobiographical, but they nearly all have this new note of quietude

and reality. Micawber is gigantic; an immense
assertion of the truth that the way to live is to
exaggerate everything. But of him I shall have to
speak more fully in another connection. Mrs.
Micawber, artistically speaking, is even better.
She is very nearly the best thing in Dickens.
Nothing could be more absurd, and at the same
time more true, than her clear argumentative
manner of speech as she sits smiling and expound-
ing in the midst of ruin. What could be more
lucid and logical and unanswerable than her statement of the prolegomena of the Medway problem,
of which the first step must be to "see the
Medway," or of the coal-trade, which required
talent and capital. "Talent Mr. Micawber has.
Capital Mr. Micawber has not." It seems as if
something should have come at last out of so clear
and scientific an arrangement of the ideas. Indeed
if (as has been suggested) we regard "David
Copperfield" as an unconscious defence of the
poetic view of life, we might regard Mrs. Micawber
as an unconscious satire on the logical view of life.
She sits as a monument of the hopelessness and
helplessness of reason in the face of this romantic
and unreasonable world.

As I have taken "Dombey and Son" as the book
before the transition, and "David Copperfield" as

typical of the transition itself, I may perhaps take "Bleak House" as the book after the transition, and so complete the description. Bleak House has every characteristic of his new realistic culture. Dickens never now, as in his early books, revels in the parts he likes and scamps the parts he does not, after the manner of Scott. He does not, as in previous tales, leave his heroes and heroines mere walking gentlemen and ladies with nothing at all to do but walk : he expends upon them at least ingenuity. By the expedients (successful or not) of the self-revelation of Esther or the humorous inconsistencies of Rick, he makes his younger figures if not lovable at least readable. Everywhere we see this tighter and more careful grip. He does not, for instance, when he wishes to denounce a dark institution, sandwich it in as a mere episode in a rambling story of adventure, as the debtor's prison is embedded in the body of Pickwick or the low Yorkshire school in the body of Nicholas Nickleby. He puts the Court of Chancery in the centre of the stage, a sombre and sinister temple, and groups round it in artistic relation decaying and fantastic figures, its offspring and its satirists. An old dipsomaniac keeps a rag and bone shop, type of futility and antiquity, and calls himself the Lord Chancellor. A little mad

old maid hangs about the courts on a forgotten or
imaginary lawsuit, and says with perfect and pungent
irony, "I am expecting a judgment shortly, on
the Day of Judgment." Rick and Ada and Esther
are not mere strollers who have strayed into the
court of law, they are its children, its symbols, and
its victims. The righteous indignation of the book
is not at the red heat of anarchy, but at the white
heat of art. Its anger is patient and plodding, like
some historic revenge. Moreover, it slowly and
carefully creates the real psychology of oppression. The endless formality, the endless unemo-
tional urbanity, the endless hope deferred, these
things make one feel the fact of injustice more than
the madness of Nero. For it is not the activeness
of tyranny that maddens, but its passiveness. We
hate the deafness of the god more than his strength.
Silence is the unbearable repartee.

Again we can see in this book strong traces of
an increase in social experience. Dickens, as his
fame carried him into more fashionable circles,
began really to understand something of what is
strong and what is weak in the English upper
class. Sir Leicester Dedlock is a far more effective condemnation of oligarchy than the ugly
swagger of Sir Mulberry Hawk, because pride
stands out more plainly in all its impotence and

insolence as the one weakness of a good man, than
as one of the million weaknesses of a bad one.
Dickens, like all young Radicals, had imagined in
his youth that aristocracy rested upon the hardness
of somebody; he found, as we all do, that it rests
upon the softness of everybody. It is very hard
not to like Sir Leicester Dedlock, not to applaud
his silly old speeches, so foolish, so manly, so
genuinely English, so disastrous to England. It
is true that the English people love a lord, but it
is not true that they fear him; rather, if anything,
they pity him; there creeps into their love something of the feeling they have towards a baby or a
black man. In their hearts they think it admirable
that Sir Leicester Dedlock should be able to
speak at all. And so a system, which no iron laws
and no bloody battles could possibly force upon
a people, is preserved from generation to generation by pure, weak good-nature.

In " Bleak House " occurs the character of
Harold Skimpole, the character whose alleged
likeness to Leigh Hunt has laid Dickens open to so
much disapproval. Unjust disapproval, I think, as
far as fundamental morals are concerned. In
method he was a little clamorous and clumsy, as,
indeed, he was apt to be. But when he said that
it was possible to combine a certain tone of

conversation taken from a particular man with other
characteristics which were not meant to be his, he
surely said what all men who write stories know.
A work of fiction often consists in combining a pair
of whiskers seen in one street with a crime seen in
another. He may quite possibly have really meant
only to make Leigh Hunt's light philosophy the
mask for a new kind of scamp, as a variant on the
pious mask of Pecksniff or the candid mask of Bagstock. He may never once have had the unfriendly
thought, "Suppose Hunt behaved like a rascal!"
he may have only had the fanciful thought, "Suppose a rascal behaved like Hunt!"

But there is a good reason for mentioning
Skimpole especially. In the character of Skimpole,
Dickens displayed again a quality that was very
admirable in him — I mean a disposition to see
things sanely and to satirize even his own faults.
He was commonly occupied in satirizing the Grad-
grinds, the economists, the men of Smiles and
Self-Help. For him there was nothing poorer than
their wealth, nothing more selfish than their self-
denial. And against them he was in the habit of
pitting the people of a more expansive habit—the
happy Swivellers and Micawbers, who, if they
were poor, were at least as rich as their last penny
could make them. He loved that great Christian

carelessness that seeks its meat from God. It
was merely a kind of uncontrollable honesty that
forced him into urging the other side. He could
not disguise from himself or from the world that
the man who began by seeking his meat from God
might end by seeking his meat from his neighbour,
without apprising his neighbour of the fact. He
had shown how good irresponsibility could be; he
could not stoop to hide how bad it could be. He
created Skimpole; and Skimpole is the dark under-
side of Micawber.

In attempting Skimpole he attempted something
with a great and urgent meaning. He attempted
it, I say; I do not assert that he carried it through.
As has been remarked, he was never successful in
describing psychological change; his characters
are the same yesterday, to-day, and for ever. And
critics have complained very justly of the crude
villainy of Skimpole's action in the matter of Joe
and Mr. Bucket. Certainly Skimpole had no need
to commit a clumsy treachery to win a clumsy
bribe; he had only to call on Mr. Jarndyce. He
had lost his honour too long to need to sell it.

The effect is bad; but I repeat that the aim was
great. Dickens wished, under the symbol of Skimpole, to point out a truth which is perhaps the most
terrible in moral psychology. I mean the fact that

it is by no means easy to draw the line between light and heavy offence. He desired to show that there are no faults, however kindly, that we can afford to flatter or to let alone; he meant that perhaps Skimpole had once been as good a man as Swiveller. If flattered or let alone, our kindliest fault can destroy our kindliest virtue. A thing may begin as a very human weakness, and end as a very inhuman weakness. Skimpole means that the extremes of evil are much nearer than we think. A man may begin by being too generous to pay his debts, and end by being too mean to pay his debts. For the vices are very strangely in league, and encourage each other. A sober man may become a drunkard through being a coward. A brave man may become a coward through being a drunkard. That is the thing Dickens was darkly trying to convey in Skimpole—that a man might become a mountain of selfishness if he attended only to the Dickens virtues. There is nothing that can be neglected; there is no such thing (he meant) as a peccadillo.

I have dwelt on this consciousness of his because, alas, it had a very sharp edge for himself. Even while he was permitting a fault originally small to make a comedy of Skimpole, a fault originally small was making a tragedy of Charles

Dickens. For Dickens also had a bad quality, not intrinsically very terrible, which he allowed to wreck his life. He also had a small weakness that could sometimes become stronger than all his strengths. His selfishness was not, it need hardly be said, the selfishness of Gradgrind; he was particularly compassionate and liberal. Nor was it in the least the selfishness of Skimpole. He was entirely self-dependent, industrious, and dignified. His selfishness was wholly a selfishness of the nerves. Whatever his whim or the temperature of the instant told him to do must be done. He was the type of man who would break a window if it would not open and give him air. And this weakness of his had, by the time of which we speak, led to a breach between himself and his wife which he was too exasperated and excited to heal in time. Everything must be put right, and put right at once, with him. If London bored him, he must go to the Continent at once; if the Continent bored him, he must come back to London at once. If the day was too noisy, the whole household must be quiet; if night was too quiet, the whole household must wake up. Above all, he had this supreme character of the domestic despot—that his good temper was, if possible, more despotic than his bad temper. When he was miserable (as he often was, poor

fellow), they only had to listen to his railings. When
he was happy they had to listen to his novels. All
this, which was mainly mere excitability, did not
seem to amount to much; it did not in the least
mean that he had ceased to be a clean-living and
kind-hearted and quite honest man. But there was
this evil about it—that he did not resist his little
weakness at all; he pampered it as Skimpole pampered his. And it separated him and his wife. A
mere silly trick of temperament did everything that
the blackest misconduct could have done. A
random sensibility, started about the shuffling of
papers or the shutting of a window, ended by tear-
ing two clean, Christian people from each other,
like a blast of bigamy or adultery.

CHAPTER IX

LATER LIFE AND WORKS

I HAVE deliberately in this book mentioned only such facts in the life of Dickens as were, I will not say significant (for all facts must be significant, including the million facts that can never be mentioned by anybody), but such facts as illustrated my own immediate meaning. I have observed this method consistently and without shame because I think that we can hardly make too evident a chasm between books which profess to be statements of all the ascertainable facts, and books which (like this one) profess only to contain a particular opinion or a summary deducible from the facts. Books like Forster's exhaustive work and others exist, and are as accessible as St. Paul's Cathedral; we have them in common as we have the facts of the physical universe; and it seems highly desirable that the function of making an exhaustive catalogue and that of making an individual generalization should not be confused. No catalogue, of course, can contain all the facts even of five minutes; every catalogue, however long

and learned, must be not only a bold, but, one may
say, an audacious selection.   But if a great many
facts are given, the reader gains a blurred belief
that all the facts are being given.   In a professedly
personal judgment it is therefore clearer and more
honest to give only a few illustrative facts,
leaving the other obtainable facts to balance them.
For thus it is made quite clear that the thing is a
sketch, an affair of a few lines

It is as well, however, to make at this point
a pause sufficient to indicate the main course of
the later life of the novelist. And it is best to
begin with the man himself, as he appeared in
those last days of popularity and public distinction.
Many are still alive who remember him in his
after-dinner speeches, his lectures, and his many
public activities ; as I am not one of these, I cannot
correct my notions with that flash of the living
features without which a description may be subtly
and entirely wrong.   Once a man is dead, if it be
only yesterday, the new-comer must piece him
together from descriptions really as much at
random as if he were describing Cæsar or Henry II.
Allowing, however, for this inevitable falsity, a
figure vivid and a little fantastic, does walk across
the stage of Forster's " Life."

Dickens was of a middle size and his vivacity

and relative physical insignificance probably gave rather the impression of small size; certainly of the absence of bulk. In early life he wore, even for that epoch, extravagant clusters of brown hair and in later years, a brown moustache and a fringe of brown beard (cut like a sort of broad and bushy imperial) sufficiently individual in shape to give him a faint air as of a foreigner. His face had a peculiar tint or quality which is hard to describe even after one has contrived to imagine it. It was the quality which Mrs. Carlyle felt to be, as it were metallic, and compared to clear steel. It was, I think, a sort of pale glitter and animation, very much alive and yet with something deathly about it, like a corpse galvanized by a god. His face (if this was so) was curiously a counterpart of his character. For the essence of all Dickens's character was that it was at once tremulous and yet hard and sharp, just as the bright blade of a sword is tremulous and yet hard and sharp. He vibrated at every touch and yet he was indestructible; you could bend him, but you could not break him. Brown of hair and beard, somewhat pale of visage (especially in his later days of excitement and ill-health) he had quite exceptionally bright and active eyes; eyes that were always darting about like brilliant birds to pick up all the tiny things of which he made more, perhaps, than any novelist has done; for he was a sort of poetical Sherlock Holmes. The mouth behind the brown beard was large and mobile, like the mouth of an actor; indeed he was an actor, in many things too much of an actor. In his lectures, in later years, he could turn his strange face into any of the innumerable mad masks that were the faces of his grotesque characters. He could make his face fall suddenly into the blank inanity of Mrs. Raddle's servant, or swell, as if to twice its size, into the apoplectic energy of Mr. Serjeant Buzfuz. But the outline of his face itself, from his youth upwards, was cut quite delicate and decisive and in repose, and in its own keen way, may even have looked effeminate.

The dress of the comfortable classes during the later years of Dickens was, compared with ours, somewhat slipshod and somewhat gaudy. It was the time of loose pegtop trousers of an almost Turkish oddity, of large ties, of loose short jackets and of loose long whiskers. Yet even this expansive period, it must be confessed, considered Dickens a little too flashy or, as some put it, too Frenchified in his dress. Such a man would wear velvet coats and wild waistcoats that were like incredible sunsets; he would wear those old white hats of an unnecessary and startling whiteness. He did not mind being seen in sensational dressing-gowns; it is said he had his portrait painted in one of them. All this is ɪnot meritorious; neither is it particularly discreditable; it is a characteristic only, but an important one. He was an absolutely independent and entirely self-respecting man. But he had none of that old lusty, half-dignified English feeling upon which Thackeray was so sensitive; I mean the desire to be regarded as a private gentleman, which means at bottom the desire to be left alone. This again is not a merit; it is only one of the milder aspects of aristocracy. But meritorious or not, Dickens did not possess it. He had no objection to being stared at, if he were also admired. He did not exactly pose in the oriental manner of Disraeli; his instincts were too clean for that; but he did pose somewhat in the French manner, of some leaders like Mirabeau and Gambetta. Nor had he the dull desire to "get on" which makes men die contented as inarticulate Under-Secretaries of State. He did not desire success so much as fame, the old human glory, the applause and wonder of the people. Such he was as he walked down the street in his Frenchified clothes, probably with a slight swagger.

His private life consisted of one tragedy and ten thousand comedies. By one tragedy I mean one real and rending moral tragedy—the failure of his marriage. He loved his children dearly, and more than one of them died; but in sorrows like these there is no violence and above all no shame. The end of life is not tragic like the end of love. And by the ten thousand comedies I mean the whole texture of his life, his letters, his conversation, which were one incessant carnival of insane and inspired improvisation. So far as he could prevent it, he never permitted a day of his life to be ordinary. There was always some prank, some impetuous proposal, some practical joke, some sudden hospitality, some sudden disappearance. It is related of him (I give one anecdote out of a hundred) that in his last visit to America, when he was already reeling as it were under the blow that was to be mortal, he remarked quite casually to his companions that a row of painted cottages looked exactly like the painted shops in a pantomime. No sooner had the suggestion passed his lips than he leapt at the nearest doorway and in exact imitation of the clown in the harlequinade, beat conscientiously with his fist, not on the door (for that would have burst the canvas scenery of course), but on the side of the doorpost. Having done this he lay down ceremoniously across the doorstep for the owner to fall over him if he should come rushing out.   He then got up gravely and went on his way. His whole life was full of such unexpected energies, precisely like those of the pantomime clown. Dickens had indeed a great and fundamental affinity with the landscape, or rather house-scape, of the harlequinade.   He liked high houses, and sloping roofs, and deep areas.   But he would have been really happy if some good fairy of the eternal pantomime had given him the power of flying off the roofs and pitching harmlessly down the height of the houses and bounding out of the areas like an indiarubber ball.   The divine lunatic in " Nicholas Nickleby" comes nearest to his dream.   I really think Dickens would rather have been that one of his characters than any of the others.   With what excitement he would have struggled down the chimney.   With what ecstatic energy he would have hurled the cucumbers over the garden wall.

His letters exhibit even more the same incessant creative force.   His letters are as creative as any of his literary creation.   His shortest postcard is often as good as his ablest novel; each one of them is spontaneous ; each one of them is different.   He varies even the form and shape of the letter as far as possible ; now it is in absurd French ; now it

is from one of his characters; now it is an advertisement for himself as a stray dog. All of them
are very funny; they are not only very funny,
but they are quite as funny as his finished and
published work. This is the ultimately amazing
thing about Dickens; the amount there is of
him. He wrote, at the very least, sixteen thick
important books packed full of original creation.
And if you had burnt them all he could have
written sixteen more, as a man writes idle letters
to his friend.

In connection with this exuberant part of his
nature there is another thing to be noted, if we are
to make a personal picture of him. Many modern
people, chiefly women, have been heard to object to
the Bacchic element in the books of Dickens, that
celebration of social drinking as a supreme symbol
of social living, which those books share with
almost all the great literature of mankind, including
the New Testament. Undoubtedly there is an
abnormal amount of drinking in a page of Dickens,
as there is an abnormal amount of fighting, say, in
a page of Dumas. If you reckon up the beers and
brandies of Mr. Bob Sawyer, with the care of an
arithmetician and the deductions of a pathologist,
they rise alarmingly like a rising tide at sea.
Dickens did defend drink clamorously, praised it

with passion, and described whole orgies of it with enormous gusto. Yet it is wonderfully typical of his prompt and impatient nature that he himself drank comparatively little. He was the type of man who could be so eager in praising the cup that he left the cup untasted. It was a part of his active and feverish temperament that he did not drink wine very much. But it was a part of his humane philosophy, of his religion, that he did drink wine. To healthy European philosophy wine is a symbol; to European religion it is a sacrament. Dickens approved it because it was a great human institution, one of the rites of civilization, and this it certainly is. The teetotaller who stands outside it may have perfectly clear ethical reasons of his own, as a man may have who stands outside education or nationality, who refuses to go to a University or to serve in an Army. But he is neglecting one of the great social things that man has added to nature. The teetotaller has chosen a most unfortunate phrase for the drunkard when he says that the drunkard is making a beast of himself. The man who drinks ordinarily makes nothing but an ordinary man of himself. The man who drinks excessively makes a devil of himself. But nothing connected with a human and artistic thing like wine can bring one nearer to the brute life of nature.

The only man who is, in the exact and literal sense
of the words, making a beast of himself is the
teetotaller.

The tone of Dickens towards religion, though
like that of most of his contemporaries, philoso-
phically disturbed and rather historically ignorant,
had an element that was very characteristic of
himself. He had all the prejudices of his time. He
had, for instance, that dislike of defined dogmas,
which really means a preference for unexamined
dogmas. He had the usual vague notion that the
whole of our human past was packed with nothing
but insane Tories. He had, in a word, all the old
Radical ignorances which went along with the old
Radical acuteness and courage and public spirit.
But this spirit tended, in almost all the others who
held it, to a specific dislike of the Church of
England; and a disposition to set the other sects
against it, as truer types of inquiry, or of individualism. Dickens had a definite tenderness for
the Church of England. He might have even called
it a weakness for the Church of England, but he
had it. Something in those placid services, something in that reticent and humane liturgy pleased
him against all the tendencies of his time; pleased
him in the best part of himself, his virile love of
charity and peace. Once, in a puff of anger at the

Church's political stupidity (which is indeed profound), he left it for a week or two and went to an
Unitarian Chapel; in a week or two he came back.
This curious and sentimental hold of the English
Church upon him increased with years. In the
book he was at work on when he died he describes
the Minor Canon, humble, chivalrous, tender-
hearted, answering with indignant simplicity the
froth and platform righteousness of the sectarian
philanthropist. He upholds Canon Crisparkle and
satirizes Mr. Honeythunder. Almost every one of
the other Radicals, his friends, would have upheld
Mr. Honeythunder and satirized Canon Crisparkle.

I have mentioned this matter for a special
reason. It brings us back to that apparent contradiction or dualism in Dickens to which, in one connection or another, I have often adverted, and
which, in one shape or another, constitutes the
whole crux of his character. I mean the union of a
general wildness approaching lunacy, with a sort
of secret moderation almost amounting to medioc-
rity. Dickens was, more or less, the man I have
described—sensitive, theatrical, amazing, a bit of a
dandy, a bit of a buffoon. Nor are such characteristics, whether weak or wild, entirely accidents or
externals. He had some false theatrical tendencies
integral in his nature. For instance, he had one

most unfortunate habit, a habit that often put him in the wrong, even when he happened to be in the right. He had an incurable habit of explaining himself. This reduced his admirers to the mental condition of the authentic but hitherto uncelebrated little girl who said to her mother, " I think I should understand if only you wouldn't explain." Dickens always would explain. It was a part of that instinctive publicity of his which made him at once a splendid democrat and a little too much of an actor. He carried it to the craziest lengths. He actually wanted to have printed, in *Punch*, it is said, an apology for his own action in the matter of his marriage. That incident alone is enough to suggest that his external offers and proposals were sometimes like screams heard from Bedlam. Yet it remains true that he had in him a central part that was pleased only by the most decent and the most reposeful rites, by things of which the Anglican Prayer-book is very typical. It is certainly true that he was often extravagant. It is most certainly equally true that he detested and despised extravagance.

The best explanation can be found in his literary genius. His literary genius consisted in a contradictory capacity at once to entertain and to deride—very ridiculous ideas. If he is a buffoon,

he is laughing at buffoonery. His books were in
some ways the wildest on the face of the world.
Rabelais did not introduce into Paphlagonia or the
Kingdom of the Coqcigrues satiric figures more
frantic and misshapen than Dickens made to walk
about the Strand and Lincoln's Inn. But for all that,
you come, in the core of him, on a sudden quietude
and good sense. Such, I think, was the core of
Rabelais, such were all the far-stretching and violent
satirists. This is a point essential to Dickens,
though very little comprehended in our current
tone of thought. Dickens was an immoderate
jester, but a moderate thinker. He was an immoderate jester because he was a moderate thinker.
What we moderns call the wildness of his imagination was actually created by what we moderns call
the tameness of his thought. I mean that he felt
the full insanity of all extreme tendencies, because
he was himself so sane; he felt eccentricities, because he was in the centre. We are always, in
these days, asking our violent prophets to write
violent satires; but violent prophets can never possibly write violent satires. In order to write satire
like that of Rabelais—satire that juggles with the
stars and kicks the world about like a football—it
is necessary to be one's self temperate, and even
mild. A modern man like Nietzsche, a modern

man like Gorky, a modern man like d'Annunzio, could not possibly write real and riotous satire. They are themselves too much on the borderlands. They could not be a success as caricaturists, for they are already a great success as caricatures.

I have mentioned his religious preference merely as an instance of this interior moderation. To say, as some have done, that he attacked Nonconformity is quite a false way of putting it. It is clean across the whole trend of the man and his time to suppose that he could have felt bitterness against any theological body as a theological body; but anything like religious extravagance, whether Protestant or Catholic, moved him to an extravagance of satire. And he flung himself into the drunken energy of Stiggins, he piled up to the stars the "verbose flights of stairs" of Mr. Chadband, exactly because his own conception of religion was the quiet and impersonal Morning Prayer. It is typical of him that he had a peculiar hatred for speeches at the grave-side.

An even clearer case of what I mean can be found in his political attitude. He seemed to some an almost anarchic satirist. He made equal fun of the systems which reformers made war on, and of the instruments on which reformers relied. He made no secret of his feeling that the average

English premier was an accidental ass. In two
superb sentences he summed up and swept away
the whole British constitution: " England, for the
last week, has been in an awful state. Lord Coodle
would go out, Sir Thomas Doodle wouldn't come
in, and there being no people in England to speak
of except Coodle and Doodle, the country has been
without a government." He lumped all cabinets
and all government offices together, and made the
same game of them all. He created his most staggering humbugs, his most adorable and incredible
idiots, and set them in the highest thrones of our
national system. To many moderate and progressive people, such a satirist seemed to be insulting
heaven and earth, ready to wreck society for
some mad alternative, prepared to pull down St.
Paul's, and on its ruins erect a gory guillotine.
Yet, as a matter of fact, this apparent wildness of
his came from his being, if anything, a very moderate politician. It came, not at all from fanaticism,
but from a rather rational detachment. He had the
sense to see that the British constitution was not
democracy, but the British constitution. It was an
artificial system—like any other, good in some
ways, bad in others. His satire of it sounded wild
to those that worshipped it; but his satire of it
arose not from his having any wild enthusiasm

against it, but simply from his not having, like
every one else, a wild enthusiasm for it. Alone, as
far as I know, among all the great Englishmen of
that age, he realized the thing that Frenchmen and
Irishmen understand. I mean the fact that popular government is one thing, and representative
government another. He realized that representative government has many minor disadvantages,
one of them being that it is never representative.
He speaks of his "hope to have made every man in
England feel something of the contempt for the
House of Commons that I have." He says also
these two things, both of which are wonderfully
penetrating as coming from a good Radical in 1855,
for they contain a perfect statement of the peril in
which we now stand, and which may, if it please
God, sting us into avoiding the long vista at the
end of which one sees so clearly the dignity and
the decay of Venice—

"I am hourly strengthened," he says, "in my
old belief, that our political aristocracy and our
tuft-hunting are the death of England. In all this
business I don't see a gleam of hope. As to the
popular spirit, it has come to be so entirely separated from the Parliament and the Government,
and so perfectly apathetic about them both, that I
seriously think it a most portentous sign." And

he says also this : " I really am serious in thinking —and I have given as painful consideration to the subject as a man with children to live and suffer after him can possibly give it—that representative government is become altogether a failure with us, that the English gentilities and subserviences render the people unfit for it, and the whole thing has broken down since the great seventeenth century time, and has no hope in it."

These are the words of a wise and perhaps melancholy man, but certainly not of an unduly excited one. It is worth noting, for instance, how much more directly Dickens goes to the point than Carlyle did, who noted many of the same evils. But Carlyle fancied that our modern English government was wordy and long-winded because it was democratic government. Dickens saw, what is certainly the fact, that it is wordy and long-winded because it is aristocratic government, the two most pleasant aristocratic qualities being a love of literature and an unconsciousness of time. But all this amounts to the same conclusion of the matter. Frantic figures like Stiggins and Chadband were created out of the quietude of his religious preference. Wild creations like the Barnacles and the Bounderbys were produced in a kind of ecstasy of the ordinary, of the obvious in political justice.

His monsters were made out of his level and his moderation, as the old monsters were made out of the level sea.

Such was the man of genius we must try to imagine; violently emotional, yet with a good judgment; pugnacious, but only when he thought himself oppressed; prone to think himself oppressed, yet not cynical about human motives. He was a man remarkably hard to understand or to reanimate. He almost always had reasons for his action; his error was that he always expounded them. Sometimes his nerve snapped; and then he was mad. Unless it did so he was quite unusually sane.

Such a rough sketch at least must suffice us in order to summarize his later years. Those years were occupied, of course, in two main additions to his previous activities. The first was the series of public readings and lectures which he now began to give systematically. The second was his successive editorship of *Household Words* and of *All the Year Round*. He was of a type that enjoys every new function and opportunity. He had been so many things in his life, a reporter, an actor, a conjurer, a poet. As he had enjoyed them all, so he enjoyed being a lecturer, and enjoyed being an editor. It is certain that his audiences (who sometimes stacked themselves so thick that they lay flat on the platform all round him) enjoyed his being a lecturer. It is not so certain that the sub-editors enjoyed his being an editor. But in both connections the main matter of importance is the effect on the permanent work of Dickens himself. The readings were important for this reason, that they fixed, as if by some public and pontifical pronouncement, what was Dickens's interpretation of Dickens's work. Such a knowledge is mere tradition, but it is very forcible. My own family has handed on to me, and I shall probably hand on to the next generation, a definite memory of how Dickens made his face suddenly like the face of an idiot in impersonating Mrs. Raddle's servant, Betsy. This does serve one of the permanent purposes of tradition ; it does make it a little more difficult for any ingenious person to prove that Betsy was meant to be a brilliant satire on the over-cultivation of the intellect.

As for his relation to his two magazines, it is chiefly important, first for the admirable things that he wrote in the magazines himself (one cannot forbear to mention the inimitable monologue of the waiter in "Somebody's Luggage"), and secondly for the fact that in his capacity of editor he made one valuable discovery. He discovered Wilkie

Collins. Wilkie Collins was the one man of unmistakable genius who has a certain affinity with
Dickens; an affinity in this respect, that they both
combine in a curious way a modern and cockney
and even commonplace opinion about things with
a huge elemental sympathy with strange oracles
and spirits and old night. There were no two men
in Mid-Victorian England, with their top-hats and
umbrellas, more typical of its rationality and dull
reform; and there were no two men who could
touch them at a ghost-story. No two men would
have more contempt for superstitions; and no two
men could so create the superstitious thrill. Indeed, our modern mystics make a mistake when
they wear long hair or loose ties to attract the
spirits. The elves and the old gods when they
revisit the earth really go straight for a dull top-
hat. For it means simplicity, which the gods love.

Meanwhile his books, appearing from time to
time, while as brilliant as ever, bore witness to
that increasing tendency to a more careful and
responsible treatment which we have remarked in
the transition which culminated in "Bleak House."
His next important book, "Hard Times," strikes
an almost unexpected note of severity. The
characters are indeed exaggerated, but they are
bitterly and deliberately exaggerated; they are not

exaggerated with the old unconscious high spirits of
Nicholas Nickleby or Martin Chuzzlewit.   Dickens
exaggerates Bounderby because he really hates him.
He exaggerated Pecksniff because he really loved
him.   "Hard Times" is not one of the greatest
books of Dickens; but it is perhaps in a sense one
of his greatest monuments.   It stamps and records
the reality of Dickens's emotion on a great many
things that were then considered unphilosophical
grumblings, but which since have swelled into the
immense phenomenon of the socialist philosophy.
To call Dickens a Socialist is a wild exaggeration ;
but the truth and peculiarity of his position might
be expressed thus : that even when everybody
thought that Liberalism meant individualism he
was emphatically a Liberal and emphatically not
an individualist.   Or the truth might be better
still stated in this manner : that he saw that there
was a secret thing, called humanity, to which both
extreme socialism and extreme individualism were
profoundly and inexpressibly indifferent, and that
this permanent and presiding humanity was the
thing he happened to understand ; he knew that
individualism is nothing and non-individualism is
nothing but the keeping of the commandment of
man.   He felt, as a novelist should, that the
question is too much discussed as to whether a

man is in favour of this or that scientific philosophy; that there is another question, whether the
scientific philosophy is in favour of the man. That
is why such books as "Hard Times" will remain
always a part of the power and tradition of Dickens.
He saw that economic systems are not things like
the stars, but things like the lamp-posts, manifestations of the human mind, and things to be judged
by the human heart.

Thenceforward until the end his books grow
consistently graver and, as it were, more responsible; he improves as an artist if not always
as a creator. "Little Dorrit" (published in 1857)
is at once in some ways so much more subtle and
in every way so much more sad than the rest of
his work that it bores Dickensians and especially
pleases George Gissing. It is the only one of the
Dickens tales which could please Gissing, not
only by its genius, but also by its atmosphere.
There is something a little modern and a little sad,
something also out of tune with the main trend
of Dickens's moral feeling, about the description
of the character of Dorrit as actually and finally
weakened by his wasting experiences, as not lifting
any cry above the conquered years. It is but a
faint fleck of shadow. But the illimitable white
light of human hopefulness, of which I spoke at

the beginning, is ebbing away, the work of the
revolution is growing weaker everywhere; and
the night of necessitarianism cometh when no man
can work. For the first time in a book by Dickens
perhaps we really do feel that the hero is forty-five.
Clennam is certainly very much older than Mr.
Pickwick.

This was indeed only a fugitive grey cloud;
he went on to breezier operations. But whatever
they were, they still had the note of the later days.
They have a more cautious craftsmanship; they
have a more mellow and a more mixed human
sentiment. Shadows fell upon his page from the
other and sadder figures out of the Victorian
decline. A good instance of this is his next book,
"The Tale of Two Cities" (1859). In dignity and
eloquence it almost stands alone among his books
by Dickens. But it also stands alone among the
books by Dickens in this respect, that it is not
entirely by Dickens. It owes its inspiration
avowedly to the passionate and cloudy pages of
Carlyle's "French Revolution." And there is
something quite essentially inconsistent between
Carlyle's disturbed and half-sceptical transcendentalism and the original school and spirit to
which Dickens belonged, the lucid and laughing
decisiveness of the old convinced and contented

Radicalism. Hence the genius of Dickens cannot save him, just as the great genius of Carlyle could not save him from making a picture of the French Revolution, which was delicately and yet deeply erroneous. Both tend too much to represent it as a mere elemental outbreak of hunger or vengeance; they do not see enough that it was a war for intellectual principles, even for intellectual platitudes. We, the modern English, cannot easily understand the French Revolution, because we cannot easily understand the idea of bloody battle for pure common sense; we cannot understand common sense in arms and conquering. In modern England common sense appears to mean putting up with existing conditions. For us a practical politician really means a man who can be thoroughly trusted to do nothing at all; that is where his practicality comes in. The French feeling—the feeling at the back of the Revolution—was that the more sensible a man was, the more you must look out for slaughter.

In all the imitators of Carlyle, including Dickens, there is an obscure sentiment that the thing for which the Frenchmen died must have been something new and queer, a paradox, a strange idolatry. But when such blood ran in the streets, it was for the sake of a truism; when those cities were shaken to their foundations, they were shaken to their foundations by a truism.

I have mentioned this historical matter because it illustrates these later and more mingled influences which at once improve and as it were perplex the later work of Dickens. For Dickens had in his original mental composition capacities for understanding this cheery and sensible element in the French Revolution far better than Carlyle. The French Revolution was, among other things, French, and, so far as that goes, could never have a precise counterpart in so jolly and autochthonous an Englishman as Charles Dickens. But there was a great deal of the actual and unbroken tradition of the Revolution itself in his early radical indictments; in his denunciations of the Fleet Prison there was a great deal of the capture of the Bastille. There, was above all, a certain reasonable impatience which was the essence of the old Republican, and which is quite unknown to the Revolutionist in modern Europe. The old Radical did not feel exactly that he was "in revolt;" he felt if anything that a number of idiotic institutions had revolted against reason and against him. Dickens, I say, had the revolutionary idea, though an English form of it, by clear and conscious inheritance; Carlyle had to rediscover the Revolution by a violence of genius and vision. If Dickens, then, took from Carlyle (as he said he did) his image of the Revolution, it does certainly mean that he had forgotten something of his own youth and come under the more complex influences of the end of the nineteenth century. His old hilarious and sentimental view of human nature seems for a moment dimmed in Little Dorrit. His old political simplicity has been slightly disturbed by Carlyle.

I repeat that this graver note is varied, but it remains a graver note. We see it struck, I think, with particular and remarkable success in "Great Expectations" (1860–61). This fine story is told with a consistency and quietude of individuality which is rare in Dickens. But so far had he travelled along the road of a heavier reality, that he even intended to give the tale an unhappy ending, making Pip lose Estella for ever; and he was only dissuaded from it by the robust romanticism of Bulwer Lytton. But the best part of the tale—the account of the vacillations of the hero between the humble life to which he owes everything, and the gorgeous life from which he expects something, touch a very true and somewhat tragic part of morals; for the great paradox of morality (the paradox to which only the religions have

given an adequate expression) is that the very
vilest kind of fault is exactly the most easy kind
We read in books and ballads about the wild fellow
who might kill a man or smoke opium, but who
would never stoop to lying or cowardice or to
"anything mean." But for actual human beings
opium and slaughter have only occasional charm;
the permanent human temptation is the temptation
to be mean. The one standing probability is the
probability of becoming a cowardly hypocrite.
The circle of the traitors is the lowest of the abyss,
and it is also the easiest to fall into. That is one of
the ringing realities of the Bible, that it does not
make its great men commit grand sins; it makes
its great men (such as David and St. Peter) commit
small sins and behave like sneaks.

Dickens has dealt with this easy descent of
desertion, this silent treason, with remarkable
accuracy in the account of the indecisions of Pip.
It contains a good suggestion of that weak romance
which is the root of all snobbishness: that the
mystery which belongs to patrician life excites
us more than the open, even the indecent virtues
of the humble. Pip is keener about Miss Havisham,
who may mean well by him, than about Joe Gargery,
who evidently does. All this is very strong and
wholesome; but it is still a little stern. "Our

Mutual Friend," 1864, brings us back a little into his merrier and more normal manner ; some of the satire, such as that upon Veneering's election, is in the best of his old style, so airy and fanciful, yet hitting so suddenly and so hard. But even here we find the fuller and more serious treatment of psychology ; notably in the two facts that he creates a really human villain, Bradley Headstone, and also one whom we might call a really human hero, Eugene, if it were not that he is much too human to be called a hero at all. It has been said (invariably by cads) that Dickens never described a gentleman ; it is like saying that he never described a zebra. A gentleman is a very rare animal among human creatures, and to people like Dickens, interested in all humanity, not a supremely important one. But in Eugene Wrayburn he does, whether consciously or not, turn that accusation with a vengeance. For he not only describes a gentleman but describes the inner weakness and peril that belong to a gentleman, the devil that is always rending the entrails of an idle and agreeable man. In Eugene's purposeless pursuit of Lizzie Hexam, in his yet more purposeless torturing of Bradley Headstone, the author has marvellously realized that singular empty obstinacy that drives the whims and pleasures of a leisured class. He sees that there is nothing that such a man more stubbornly adheres to, than the thing that he does not particularly want to do. We are still in serious psychology.

His last book represents yet another new departure, dividing him from the chaotic Dickens of days long before. His last book is not merely an attempt to improve his power of construction in a story : it is an attempt to rely entirely on that power of construction. It not only has a plot, it is a plot. "The Mystery of Edwin Drood," 1870, was in such a sense, perhaps, the most ambitious book that Dickens ever attempted. It is, as every one knows, a detective story, and certainly a very successful one, as is attested by the tumult of discussion as to its proper solution. In this, quite apart from its unfinished state, it stands, I think, alone among the author's works. Elsewhere, if he introduced a mystery, he seldom took the trouble to make it very mysterious. "Our Mutual Friend" was finished, but if only half of it were readable, I think any one could see that John Rokesmith was John Harman. "Bleak House" is finished, but if it were only half finished I think any one would guess that Lady Dedlock and Nemo had sinned in the past. "Edwin Drood" is not finished ; for in the very middle of it Dickens died.

He had altogether overstrained himself in a last lecturing tour in America. He was a man in whom any serious malady would naturally make very rapid strides; for he had the temper of an irrational invalid. I have said before that there was in his curious character something that was feminine. Certainly there was nothing more entirely feminine than this, that he worked because he was tired. Fatigue bred in him a false and feverish industry, and his case increased, like the case of a man who drinks to cure the effects of drink. He died in 1870; and the whole nation mourned him as no public man has ever been mourned; for prime ministers and princes were private persons compared with Dickens. He had been a great popular king, like a king of some more primal age whom his people could come and see, giving judgment under an oak tree. He had in essence held great audiences of millions, and made proclamations to more than one of the nations of the earth. His obvious omnipresence in every part of public life was like the omnipresence of the sovereign. His secret omnipresence in every house and hut of private life was more like the omnipresence of a diety. Compared with that popular leadership all the fusses of the last forty years are diversions in idleness. Compared with such a case as his it may be said that we play with our politicians, and manage to endure our authors. We shall never have again such a popularity until we have again a people.

He left behind him this almost sombre fragment, "the Mystery of Edwin Drood." As one turns it over the tragic element of its truncation mingles somewhat with an element of tragedy in the thing itself; the passionate and predestined Landless, or the half maniacal Jasper carving devils out of his own heart. The workmanship of it is very fine; the right hand has not only not lost, but is still gaining its cunning. But as we turn the now enigmatic pages the thought creeps into us again which I have suggested earlier, and which is never far off the mind of a true lover of Dickens. Had he lost or gained by the growth of technique and probability in his later work? His later characters were more like men; but were not his earlier characters more like immortals? He has become able to perform a social scene so that it is possible at any rate; but where is that Dickens who once performed the impossible? Where is that young poet who created such majors and architects as Nature will never dare to create? Dickens learnt to describe daily life as Thackeray and Jane Austen could describe it; but Thackeray

could not have thought such a thought as Crummles;
and it is painful to think of Miss Austen attempting to imagine Mantalini.   After all, we feel there
are many able novelists; but there is only one
Dickens, and whither has he fled?

He was alive to the end.   And in this last dark
and secretive story of Edwin Drood he makes one
splendid and staggering appearance, like a magi-
cian saying farewell to mankind.   In the centre of
this otherwise reasonable and rather melancholy
book, this grey story of a good clergyman and the
quiet Cloisterham Towers, Dickens has calmly
inserted one entirely delightful and entirely insane
passage.   I mean the frantic and inconceivable
epitaph of Mrs. Sapsea, that which describes her
as "the reverential wife" of Thomas Sapsea,
speaks of her consistency in "looking up to him,"
and ends with the words, spaced out so admirably
on the tombstone, "Stranger pause.   And ask thy-
self this question, Canst thou do likewise?   If not,
with a blush retire."   Not the wildest tale in
Pickwick contains such an impossibility as that;
Dickens dare scarcely have introduced it, even as
one of Jingle's lies.   In no human churchyard will
you find that invaluable tombstone; indeed, you
could scarcely find it in any world where there
are churchyards.   You could scarcely have such

immortal folly as that in a world where there is also death.   Mr. Sapsea is one of the golden things stored up for us in a better world.

Yes, there were many other Dickenses : a clever Dickens, an industrious Dickens, a public-spirited Dickens; but this was the great one.   This last outbreak of insane humour reminds us wherein lay his power and his supremacy.   The praise of such beatific buffoonery should be the final praise, the ultimate word in his honour.   The wild epitaph of Mrs. Sapsea should be the serious epitaph of Dickens.

CHAPTER X

THE GREAT DICKENS CHARACTERS

ALL criticism tends too much to become criticism of criticism; and the reason is very evident. It is that criticism of creation is so very staggering a thing. We see this in the difficulty of criticizing any artistic creation. We see it again in the difficulty of criticizing that creation which is spelt with a capital C. The pessimists who attack the Universe are always under this disadvantage. They have an exhilarating consciousness that they could make the sun and moon better; but they also have the depressing consciousness that they could not make the sun and moon at all. A man looking at a hippopotamus may sometimes be tempted to regard a hippopotamus as an enormous mistake; but he is also bound to confess that a fortunate inferiority prevents him personally from making such mistakes. It is neither a blasphemy nor an exaggeration to say that we feel something of the same difficulty in judging of the very creative element in human literature.

And this is the first and last dignity of Dickens ; that he was a creator. He did not point out things, he made them. We may disapprove of Mr. Guppy, but we recognize him as a creation flung down like a miracle out of an upper sphere ; we can pull him to pieces, but we could not have put him together. We can destroy Mrs. Gamp in our wrath, but we could not have made her in our joy. Under this disadvantage any book about Dickens must definitely labour. Real primary creation (such as the sun or the birth of a child) calls forth not criticism, not appreciation, but a kind of incoherent gratitude. This is why most hymns about God are bad ; and this is why most eulogies on Dickens are bad. The eulogists of the divine and of the human creator are alike inclined to appear sentimentalists because they are talking about something so very real. In the same way love-letters always sound florid and artificial because they are about something real.

Any chapter such as this chapter must therefore in a sense be inadequate. There is no way of dealing properly with the ultimate greatness of Dickens, except by offering sacrifice to him as a god ; and this is opposed to the etiquette of our time. But something can perhaps be done in the way of suggesting what was the quality of this creation. But even in considering its quality we ought to remember that quality is not the whole question. One of the godlike things about Dickens is his quantity, his quantity as such, the enormous output, the incredible fecundity of his invention. I have said a moment ago that not one of us could have invented Mr. Guppy. But even if we could have stolen Mr. Guppy from Dickens we have still to confront the fact that Dickens would have been able to invent another quite inconceivable character to take his place. Perhaps we could have created Mr. Guppy; but the effort would certainly have exhausted us; we should be ever afterwards wheeled about in a bath-chair at Bournemouth.

Nevertheless there is something that is worth saying about the quality of Dickens. At the very beginning of this review I remarked that the reader must be in a mood, at least, of democracy. To some it may have sounded irrelevant; but the Revolution was as much behind all the books of the nineteenth century as the Catholic religion (let us say) was behind all the colours and carving of the Middle Ages. Another great name of the nineteenth century will afford an evidence of this; and will also bring us most sharply to the problem of the literary quality of Dickens.

Of all these nineteenth-century writers there

is none, in the noblest sense, more democratic than
Walter Scott. As this may be disputed, and as
it is relevant, I will expand the remark. There
are two rooted spiritual realities out of which
grow all kinds of democratic conception or
sentiment of human equality. There are two
things in which all men are manifestly and unmis-
takably equal. They are not equally clever or
equally muscular or equally fat, as the sages of
the modern reaction (with piercing insight) perceive. But this is a spiritual certainty, that all
men are tragic. And this again, is an equally
sublime spiritual certainty, that all men are comic.
No special and private sorrow can be so dreadful
as the fact of having to die. And no freak or
deformity can be so funny as the mere fact of
having two legs. Every man is important if he
loses his life; and every man is funny if he loses
his hat, and has to run after it. And the universal
test everywhere of whether a thing is popular, of
the people, is whether it employs vigorously these
extremes of the tragic and the comic. Shelley, for
instance, was an aristocrat, if ever there was one
in this world. He was a Republican, but he was
not a democrat : in his poetry there is every perfect
quality except this pungent and popular stab. For
the tragic and the comic you must go, say, to

Burns, a poor man. And all over the world, the folk literature, the popular literature, is the same. It consists of very dignified sorrow and very undignified fun. Its sad tales are of broken hearts ; its happy tales are of broken heads.

These, I say, are two roots of democratic reality. But they have in more civilized literature, a more civilized embodiment or form. In literature such as that of the nineteenth century the two elements appear somewhat thus. Tragedy becomes a profound sense of human dignity. The other and jollier element becomes a delighted sense of human variety. The first supports equality by saying that all men are equally sublime. The second supports equality by observing that all men are equally interesting.

In this democratic aspect of the interest and variety of all men, there is, of course, no democrat so great as Dickens. But in the other matter, in the idea of the dignity of all men, I repeat that there is no democrat so great as Scott. This fact, which is the moral and enduring magnificence of Scott, has been astonishingly overlooked. His rich and dramatic effects are gained in almost every case by some grotesque or beggarly figure rising into a human pride and rhetoric. The common man, in the sense of the paltry man, becomes the common man in the sense of the universal man. He declares his humanity. For the meanest of all the modernities has been the notion that the heroic is an oddity or variation, and that the things that unite us are merely flat or foul. The common things are terrible and startling, death, for instance, and first love: the things that are common are the things that are not commonplace. Into such high and central passions the comic Scott character will suddenly rise. Remember the firm and almost stately answer of the preposterous Nicol Jarvie when Helen Macgregor seeks to browbeat him into condoning lawlessness and breaking his bourgeois decency. That speech is a great monument of the middle class. Molière made M. Jourdain talk prose; but Scott made him talk poetry. Think of the rising and rousing voice of the dull and gluttonous Athelstane when he answers and overwhelms De Bracy. Think of the proud appeal of the old beggar in the "Antiquary" when he rebukes the duellists. Scott was fond of describing kings in disguise. But all his characters are kings in disguise. He was, with all his errors, profoundly possessed with the old religious conception, the only possible democratic basis, the idea that man himself is a king in disguise.

In all this Scott, though a Royalist and a Tory, had in the strangest way, the heart of the Revolution. For instance, he regarded rhetoric, the art of the orator, as the immediate weapon of the oppressed. All his poor men make grand speeches, as they did in the Jacobin Club, which Scott would have so much detested. And it is odd to reflect that he was, as an author, giving free speech to fictitious rebels while he was, as a stupid politician, denying it to real ones. But the point for us here is this : that all this popular sympathy of his rests on the graver basis, on the dark dignity of man. "Can you find no way?" asks Sir Arthur Wardour of the beggar when they are cut off by the tide. "I'll give you a farm . . . I'll make you rich." . . . "Our riches will soon be equal," says the beggar, and looks out across the advancing sea.

Now, I have dwelt on this strong point of Scott because it is the best illustration of the one weak point of Dickens. Dickens had little or none of this sense of the concealed sublimity of every separate man. Dickens's sense of democracy was entirely of the other kind ; it rested on the other of the two supports of which I have spoken. It rested on the sense that all men were wildly interesting and wildly varied. When a Dickens character becomes excited he becomes more and more himself.

He does not, like the Scott beggar, turn more and more into man. As he rises he grows more and more into a gargoyle or grotesque. He does not, like the fine speaker in Scott, grow more classical as he grows more passionate, more universal as he grows more intense. The thing can only be illustrated by a special case. Dickens did more than once, of course, make one of his quaint or humble characters assert himself in a serious crisis or defy the powerful. There is, for instance, the quite admirable scene in which Susan Nipper (one of the greatest of Dickens's achievements) faces and rebukes Mr. Dombey. But it is still true (and quite appropriate in its own place and manner) that Susan Nipper remains a purely comic character throughout her speech, and even grows more comic as she goes on. She is more serious than usual in her meaning, but not more serious in her style. Dickens keeps the natural diction of Nipper, but makes her grow more Nipperish as she grows more warm. But Scott keeps the natural diction of Baillie Jarvie, but insensibly sobers and uplifts that style until it reaches a plain and appropriate eloquence. This plain and appropriate eloquence was (except in a few places at the end of "Pickwick") almost unknown to Dickens. Whenever he made comic characters talk sentiment comically,

as in the instance of Susan, it was a success, but
an avowedly extravagant success. Whenever he
made comic characters talk sentiment seriously it
was an extravagant failure. Humour was his
medium; his only way of approaching emotion.
Wherever you do not get humour, you get unconscious humour.

As I have said elsewhere in this book Dickens
was deeply and radically English; the most English
of our great writers. And there is something very
English in this contentment with a grotesque
democracy; and in this absence of the eloquence
and elevation of Scott. The English democracy is
the most humorous democracy in the world. The
Scotch democracy is the most dignified, while the
whole abandon and satiric genius of the English
populace come from its being quite undignified in
every way. A comparison of the two types might
be found, for instance, by putting a Scotch Labour
Leader like Mr. Keir Hardie alongside an English
Labour Leader like Mr. Will Crooks. Both are good
men, honest, and responsible and compassionate;
but we can feel that the Scotchman carries himself
seriously and universally, the Englishman personally and with an obstinate humour. Mr. Keir Hardie
wishes to hold up his head as Man, Mr. Crooks
wishes to follow his nose as Crooks. Mr. Keir

Hardie is very like a poor man in Walter Scott. Mr. Crooks is very like a poor man in Dickens.

Dickens then had this English feeling of a grotesque democracy. By that is more properly meant a vastly varying democracy. The intoxicating variety of men—that was his vision and conception of human brotherhood. And certainly it is a great part of human brotherhood. In one sense things can only be equal if they are entirely different. Thus, for instance, people talk with a quite astonishing gravity about the inequality or equality of the sexes; as if there could possibly be any inequality between a lock and a key. Wherever there is no element of variety, wherever all the items literally have an identical aim, there is at once and of necessity inequality. A woman is only inferior to man in the matter of being not so manly; she is inferior in nothing else. Man is inferior to woman in so far as he is not a woman; there is no other reason. And the same applies in some degree to all genuine differences. It is a great mistake to suppose that love unites and unifies men. Love diversifies them, because love is directed towards individuality. The thing that really unites men and makes them like to each other is hatred. Thus, for instance, the more we love Germany the more pleased we shall be that

Germany should be something different from ourselves, should keep her own ritual and conviviality and we ours. But the more we hate Germany the more we shall copy German guns and German fortifications in order to be armed against Germany. The more modern nations detest each other the more meekly they follow each other; for all competition is in its nature only a furious plagiarism. As competion means always similarity, it is equally true that similarity always means inequality. If everything is trying to be green, some things will be greener than others; but there is an immortal and indestructible equality between green and red. Something of the same kind of irrefutable equality exists between the violent and varying creations of such a writer as Dickens. They are all equally ecstatic fulfilments of a separate line of development. It would be hard to say that there could be any comparison or inequality, let us say between Mr. Sapsea and Mr. Elijah Pogram. They are both in the same difficulty; they can neither of them contrive to exist in this world; they are both too big for the gate of birth.

Of the high virtue of this variation I shall speak more adequately in a moment; but certainly this love of mere variation (which I have contrasted with the classicism of Scott) is the only intelligent statement of the common case against the exaggeration of Dickens. This is the meaning, the only sane or endurable meaning, which people have in their minds when they say that Dickens is a mere caricaturist. They do not mean merely that Uncle Pumblechook does not exist. A fictitious character ought not to be a person who exists ; he ought to be an entirely new combination, an addition to the creatures already existing on the earth. They do not mean that Uncle Pumblechook could not exist ; for on that obviously they can have no knowledge whatever. They do not mean that Uncle Pumblechook's utterances are selected and arranged so as to bring out his essential Pumblechookery ; to say that is simply to say that he occurs in a work of art. But what they do really mean is this, and there is an element of truth in it. They mean that Dickens nowhere makes the reader feel that Pumblechook has any kind of fundamental human dignity at all. It is nowhere suggested that Pumblechook will some day die. He is felt rather as one of the idle and evil fairies, who are innocuous and yet malignant, and who live for ever because they never really live at all. This dehumanized vitality, this fantasy, this irresponsibility of creation, does in some sense truly belong to Dickens. It is the lower side of his hilarious human variety. But

now we come to the higher side of his human
variety, and it is far more difficult to state.

Mr. George Gissing, from the point of view of
the passing intellectualism of our day, has made
(among his many wise tributes to Dickens) a characteristic complaint about him. He has said that
Dickens, with all his undoubted sympathy for the
lower classes, never made a working man, a poor
man, specifically and highly intellectual. An exception does exist, which he must at least have
realized—a wit, a diplomatist, a great philosopher.
I mean, of course, Mr. Weller. Broadly, however,
the accusation has a truth, though it is a truth that
Mr. Gissing did not grasp in its entirety. It is not
only true that Dickens seldom made a poor character what we call intellectual; it is also true that he
seldom made any character what we call intellectual. Intellectualism was not at all present to
his imagination. What was present to his imagination was character—a thing which is not only more
important than intellect, but is also much more
entertaining. When some English moralists write
about the importance of having character, they
appear to mean only the importance of having a
dull character. But character is brighter than wit,
and much more complex than sophistry. The
whole superiority of the democracy of Dickens

over the democracy of such a man as Gissing lies
exactly in the fact that Gissing would have liked to
prove that poor men could instruct themselves and
could instruct others. It was of final importance
to Dickens that poor men could amuse themselves
and could amuse him. He troubled little about the
mere education of that life ; he declared two essential things about it—that it was laughable, and that
it was livable. The humble characters of Dickens
do not amuse each other with epigrams; they
amuse each other with themselves. The present
that each man brings in hand is his own incredible
personality. In the most sacred sense, and in the
most literal sense of the phrase, he "gives himself
away." Now, the man who gives himself away
does the last act of generosity ; he is like a martyr,
a lover, or a monk. But he is also almost certainly
what we commonly call a fool.

The key of the great characters of Dickens is
that they are all great fools. There is the same
difference between a great fool and a small fool
as there is between a great poet and a small poet.
The great fool is a being who is above wisdom
rather than below it. That element of greatness of
which I spoke at the beginning of this book is
nowhere more clearly indicated than in such
characters. A man can be entirely great while he

is entirely foolish. We see this in the epic heroes, such as Achilles. Nay, a man can be entirely great because he is entirely foolish. We see this in all the great comic characters of all the great comic writers of whom Dickens was the last. Bottom the Weaver is great because he is foolish ; Mr Toots is great because he is foolish. The thing I mean can be observed, for instance, in innumerable actual characters. Which of us has not known, for instance, a great rustic ?—a character so incurably characteristic that he seemed to break through all canons about cleverness or stupidity ; we do not know whether he is an enormous idiot or an enormous philosopher ; we know only that he is enormous, like a hill. These great, grotesque characters are almost entirely to be found where Dickens found them—among the poorer classes. The gentry only attain this greatness by going slightly mad. But who has not known an un-fathomably personal old nurse? Who has not known an abysmal butler? The truth is that our public life consists almost exclusively of small men. Our public men are small because they have to prove that they are in the common-place interpretation clever, because they have to pass examinations, to learn codes of manners, to imitate a fixed type. It is in private life that we

find the great characters. They are too great
to get into the public world. It is easier for a
camel to pass through the eye of a needle than for
a great man to enter into the kingdoms of the
earth. The truly great and gorgeous personality,
he who talks as no one else could talk and feels
with an elementary fire, you will never find this
man on any cabinet bench, in any literary circle,
at any society dinner. Least of all will you find
him in artistic society; he is utterly unknown
in Bohemia. He is more than clever, he is
amusing. He is more than successful, he is alive.
You will find him stranded here and there in all
sorts of unknown positions, almost always in unsuccessful positions. You will find him adrift as
an impecunious commercial traveller like Micawber.
You will find him but one of a batch of silly clerks,
like Swiveller. You will find him as an unsuccessful actor, like Crummles. You will find him as an
unsuccessful doctor, like Sawyer. But you will
always find this rich and reeking personality where
Dickens found it—among the poor. For the glory
of this world is a very small and priggish affair,
and these men are too large to get in line with it.
They are too strong to conquer.

It is impossible to do justice to these figures
because the essential of them is their multiplicity.

The whole point of Dickens is that he not only made them, but made them by myriads; that he stamped his foot, and armies came out of the earth. But let us, for the sake of showing the true Dickens method, take one of them, a very sublime one, Toots. It affords a good example of the real work of Dickens, which was the revealing of a certain grotesque greatness inside an obscure and even unattractive type. It reveals the great paradox of all spiritual things; that the inside is always larger than the outside.

Toots is a type that we all know as well as we know chimney-pots. And of all conceivable human figures he is apparently the most futile and the most dull. He is the blockhead who hangs on at a private school, overgrown and underdeveloped. He is always backward in his lessons, but forward in certain cheap ways of the world; he can smoke before he can spell. Toots is a perfect and pungent picture of the wretched youth. Toots has, as this youth always has, a little money of his own; enough to waste in a semi-dissipation he does not enjoy, and in a gaping regard for sports in which he could not possibly excell. Toots has, as this youth always has, bits of surreptitious finery, in his case the incomparable ring. In Toots, above all, is exactly rendered the central and most startling

contradiction; the contrast between a jauntiness
and a certain impudence of the attire, with the
profou. J shame and sheepishness of the visage and
the ch racter. In him, too, is expressed the larger
contr. .t between the external gaiety of such a lad's
occupations, and the infinite, disconsolate sadness
of his empty eyes. This is Toots; we know him,
we pity him, and we avoid him. Schoolmasters
deal with him in despair or in a heart-breaking
patience. His family is vague about him. His
low-class hangers-on (like the Game Chicken) lead
him by the nose. The very parasites that live on
him despise him. But Dickens does not despise
him. Without denying one of the dreary details
which make us avoid the man, Dickens makes him
a man whom we long to meet. He does not gloss
over one of his dismal deficiencies, but he makes
them seem suddenly like violent virtues that we
would go to the world's end to see. Without
altering one fact, he manages to alter the whole
atmosphere, the whole universe of Toots. He
makes us not only like, but love, not only love, but
reverence this little dunce and cad. The power to
do this is a power truly and literally to be called
divine.

For this is the very wholesome point. Dickens
does not alter Toots in any vital point. The thing

he does alter is us. He makes us lively where we
were bored, kind where we were cruel, and above
all, free for an universal human laughter where we
were cramped in a small competition about that sad
and solemn thing, the intellect. His enthusiasm
fills us, as does the love of God, with a glorious
shame; after all, he has only found in Toots what
we might have found for ourselves. He has only
made us as much interested in Toots as Toots is in
himself. He does not alter the proportions of
Toots; he alters only the scale; we seem as if we
were staring at a rat risen to the stature of an
elephant. Hitherto we have passed him by; now
we feel that nothing could induce us to pass him
by; that is the nearest way of putting the truth.
He has not been whitewashed in the least; he has
not been depicted as any cleverer than he is. He
has been turned from a small fool into a great fool.
We know Toots is not clever; but we are not
inclined to quarrel with Toots because he is not
clever. We are more likely to quarrel with cleverness because it is not Toots. All the examinations
he could not pass, all the schools he could not enter,
all the temporary tests of brain and culture which
surrounded him shall pass, and Toots shall remain
like a mountain.

It may be noticed that the great artists always

choose great fools 'rather than great intellectuals
to embody humanity.   Hamlet does express the
æsthetic dreams and the bewilderments of the
intellect; but Bottom the Weaver expresses them
much better.   In the same manner Toots expresses
certain permanent dignities in human nature more
than any of Dickens's more dignified characters can
do it.   For instance, Toots expresses admirably
the enduring fear, which is the very essence of
falling in love.   When Toots is invited by Florence
to come in, when he longs to come in, but still stays
out, he is embodying a sort of insane and perverse
humility which is elementary in the lover.

There is an apostolic injunction to suffer fools
gladly.   We always lay the stress on the word
"suffer," and interpret the passage as one urging
resignation.   It might be better, perhaps, to lay
the stress upon the word "gladly," and make our
familiarity with fools a delight, and almost a dissi-
pation.   Nor is it necessary that our pleasure in
fools (or at least in great and godlike fools) should
be merely satiric or cruel.   The great fool is he in
whom we cannot tell which is the conscious and
which the unconscious humour; we laugh with
him and laugh at him at the same time.   An
obvious instance is that of ordinary and happy
marriage.   A man and a woman cannot live

together without having against each other a kind
of everlasting joke. Each has discovered that the
other is a fool, but a great fool. This largeness,
this grossness and gorgeousness of folly is the
thing which we all find about those with whom we
are in intimate contact; and it is the one enduring
basis of affection, and even of respect. When we
know an individual named Tomkins, we know that
he has succeeded where all others have failed; he
has succeeded in being Tomkins. Just so Mr.
Toots succeeded; he was defeated in all scholastic
examinations, but he was the victor in that visionary
battle in which unknown competitors vainly tried
to be Toots.

If we are to look for lessons, here at least is the
last and deepest lesson of Dickens. It is in our
own daily life that we are to look for the portents
and the prodigies. This is the truth, not merely
of the fixed figures of our life; the wife, the husband,
the fool that fills the sky. It is true of the whole
stream and substance of our daily experience;
every instant we reject a great fool merely because
he is foolish. Every day we neglect Tootses and
Swivellers, Guppys and Joblings, Simmerys and
Flashers. Every day we lose the last sight of
Jobling and Chuckster, the Analytical Chemist, or
the Marchioness. Every day we are missing a

monster whom we might easily love, and an imbecile whom we should certainly admire. This is the real gospel of Dickens; the inexhaustible opportunities offered by the liberty and the variety of man. Compared with this life, all public life, all fame, all wisdom, is by its nature cramped and cold and small. For on that defined and lighted public stage men are of necessity forced to profess one set of accomplishments, to rise to one rigid standard. It is the utterly unknown people, who can grow in all directions like an exuberant tree. It is in our interior lives that we find that people are too much themselves. It is in our private life that we find people intolerably individual, that we find them swelling into the enormous contours, and taking on the colours of caricature. Many of us live publicly with featureless public puppets, images of the small public abstractions. It is when we pass our own private gate, and open our own secret door, that we step into the land of the giants.

CHAPTER XI

ON THE ALLEGED OPTIMISM OF DICKENS

IN one of the plays of the decadent period, an intellectual expressed the atmosphere of his epoch by referring to Dickens as "a vulgar optimist." I have in a previous chapter suggested something of the real strangeness of such a term. After all, the main matter of astonishment (or rather of admiration) is that optimism should be vulgar. In a world in which physical distress is almost the common lot, we actually complain that happiness is too common. In a world in which the majority is physically miserable we actually complain of the sameness of praise; we are bored with the abundance of approval. When we consider what the conditions of the vulgar really are, it is difficult to imagine a stranger or more splendid tribute to humanity than such a phrase as vulgar optimism. It is as if one spoke of "vulgar martyrdom" or "common crucifixion."

First, however, let it be said frankly that there is a foundation for the charge against Dickens which is implied in the phrase about vulgar optimism. It does not concern itself with Dickens' confidence in the value of existence and the intrinsic victory of virtue; that is not optimism but religion. Is it not concerned with his habit of making bright occasions bright, and happy stories happy, that is not optimism, but literature. Nor is it concerned even with his peculiar genius for the description of an almost bloated joviality; that is not optimism, it is simply Dickens. With all these higher variations of optimism I deal elsewhere. But over and above all these there is a real sense in which Dickens laid himself open to the accusation of a vulgar optimism, and I desire to put the admission of this first, before the discussion that follows. Dickens did have a disposition to make his characters at all costs happy, or, to speak more strictly, he had a disposition to make them comfortable rather than happy. He had a sort of literary hospitality; he too often treated his characters as if they were his guests. From a host is always expected, and always ought to be expected as long as human civilization is healthy, a strictly physical benevolence, if you will, a kind of coarse benevolence. Food and fire and such things should always be the symbols of the man entertaining men; because they are the things which all men beyond question have in common. But something more than this is needed from the man who is imagining and making men, the artist, the man who is not receiving men, but rather sending them forth.

As I shall remark in a moment in the matter of the Dickens villains, it is not true that he made every one thus at home. But he did do it to a certain wide class of incongruous characters; he did it to all who had been in any way unfortunate. It had indeed its origin (a very beautiful origin) in his realization of how much a little pleasure was to such people. He knew well that the greatest happiness that has been known since Eden is the happiness of the unhappy. So far he is admirable. And as long as he was describing the ecstasy of the poor, the borderland between pain and pleasure, he was at his highest. Nothing that has ever been written about human delights, no Earthly Paradise, no Utopia has ever come so near the quick nerve of happiness as his descriptions of the rare extravagances of the poor; such an admirable description, for instance, as that of Kit Nubbles taking his family to the theatre. For he seizes on the real source of the whole pleasure; a holy fear. Kit tells the waiter to bring the beer. And the waiter, instead of saying, "Did you address that language to me," said, "Pot of beer, sir; yes, sir." That internal and quivering humility of Kit is the only way to enjoy life or banquets; and the fear of the waiter is the beginning of dining. People in this mood "take their pleasures sadly;" which is the only way of taking them at all.

So far Dickens is supremely right. As long as he was dealing with such penury and such festivity his touch was almost invariably sure. But when he came to more difficult cases, to people who for one reason or another could not be cured with one good dinner, he did develop this other evil, this genuinely vulgar optimism of which I speak. And the mark of it is this: that he gave the characters a comfort that had no especial connection with themselves; he threw comfort at them like alms. There are cases at the end of his stories in which his kindness to his characters is a careless and insolent kindness. He loses his real charity and adopts the charity of the Charity Organization Society; the charity that is not kind, the charity that is puffed up, and that does behave itself unseemly. At the end of some of his stories he deals out his characters a kind of out-door relief.

I will give two instances. The whole meaning of the character of Mr. Micawber is that a man can be always almost rich by constantly expecting riches. The lesson is a really important one in our sweeping modern sociology. We talk of the

man whose life is a failure; but Micawber's life
never is a failure, because it is always a crisis.
We think constantly of the man who if he looked
back would see that his existence was unsuccessful; but Micawber never does look back; he
always looks forward, because the bailiff is coming
to-morrow. You cannot say he is defeated, for his
absurd battle never ends; he cannot despair of life,
for he is so much occupied in living. All this is
of immense importance in the understanding of the
poor; it is worth all the slum novelists that ever
insulted democracy. But how did it happen, how
could it happen, that the man who created this
Micawber could pension him off at the end of
the story and make him a successful colonial
mayor? Micawber never did succeed, never ought
to succeed; his kingdom is not of this world. But
this is an excellent instance of Dickens's disposition
to make his characters grossly and incongruously
comfortable. There is another instance in the
same book. Dora, the first wife of David Copperfield, is a very genuine and amusing figure; she
has certainly far more force of character than
Agnes. She represents the infinite and divine
irrationality of the human heart. What possessed
Dickens to make her such a dehumanized prig as
to recommend her husband to marry another

woman? One could easily respect a husband who after time and development made such a marriage, but surely not a wife who desired it. If Dora had died hating Agnes we should know that everything was right, and that God would reconcile the irreconcilable. When Dora dies recommending Agnes we know that everything is wrong, at least if hypocrisy and artificiality and moral vulgarity are wrong. There, again, Dickens yields to a mere desire to give comfort. He wishes to pile up pillows round Dora; and he smothers her with them, like Othello.

This is the real vulgar optimism of Dickens; it does exist, and I have deliberately put it first. Let us admit that Dickens's mind was far too much filled with pictures of satisfaction and cosiness and repose. Let us admit that he thought principally of the pleasures of the oppressed classes; let us admit that it hardly cost him any artistic pang to make out human beings as much happier than they are. Let us admit all this, and a curious fact remains.

For it was this too easily contented Dickens, this man with cushions at his back and (it sometimes seems) cotton wool in his ears, it was this happy dreamer, this vulgar optimist who alone of modern writers did really destroy some of the wrongs he hated and bring about some of the reforms he desired. Dickens did help to pull down the debtors' prisons; and if he was too much of an optimist he was quite enough of a destroyer. Dickens did drive Squeers out of his Yorkshire den; and if Dickens was too contented, it was more than Squeers was. Dickens did leave his mark on parochialism, on nursing, on funerals, on public executions, on workhouses, on the Court of Chancery. These things were altered; they are different. It may be that such reforms are not adequate remedies; that is another question altogether. The next sociologists may think these old Radical reforms quite narrow or accidental. But such as they were, the old radicals got them done; and the new sociologists cannot get anything done at all. And in the practical doing of them Dickens played a solid and quite demonstrable part; that is the plain matter that concerns us here. If Dickens was an optimist he was an uncommonly active and useful kind of optimist. If Dickens was a sentimentalist he was a very practical sentimentalist.

And the reason of this is one that goes deep into Dickens's social reform, and like every other real and desirable thing, involves a kind of mystical contradiction. If we are to save the oppressed, we must have two apparently antagonistic emotions in us at the same time. We must think the oppressed man intensely miserable, and at the same time intensely attractive and important. We must insist with violence upon his degradation; we must insist with the same violence upon his dignity. For if we relax by one inch the one assertion, men will say he does not need saving. And if we relax by one inch the other assertion, men will say he is not worth saving. The optimists will say that reform is needless. The pessimists will say that reform is hopeless. We must apply both simultaneously to the same oppressed man; we must say that he is a worm and a god; and we must thus lay ourselves open to the accusation (or the compliment) of transcendentalism. This is, indeed, the strongest argument for the religious conception of life. If the dignity of man is an earthly dignity we shall be tempted to deny his earthly degradation. If it is a heavenly dignity we can admit the earthly degradation with all the candour of Zola. If we are idealists about the other world we can be realists about this world. But that is not here the point. What is quite evident is that if a logical praise of the poor man is pushed too far, and if a logical distress about him is pushed too far, either will involve wreckage to the central paradox of reform. If the poor man is made too admirable he ceases to be pitiable ; if the poor man is made too pitiable he becomes merely contemptible. There is a school of smug optimists who will deny that he is a poor man. There is a school of scientific pessimists who will deny that he is a man.

Out of this perennial contradiction arises the fact that there are always two types of the reformer. The first we may call for convenience the pessimistic, the second the optimistic reformer. One dwells upon the fact that souls are being lost ; the other dwells upon the fact that they are worth saving. Both, of course, are (so far as that is concerned) quite right, but they naturally tend to a difference of method, and sometimes to a difference of perception. The pessimistic reformer points out the good elements that oppression has destroyed ; the optimistic reformer, with an even fiercer joy, points out the good elements that it has not destroyed. It is the case for the first reformer that slavery has made men slavish. It is the case for the second reformer that slavery has not made men slavish. The first describes how bad men are under bad conditions. The second describes how good men are under bad conditions. Of the first class of writers, for instance, is Gorky. Of the second class of writers is Dickens.

But here we must register a real and somewhat startling fact. In the face of all apparent probability, it is certainly true that the optimistic reformer reforms much more completely than the pessimistic reformer. People produce violent changes by being contented, by being far too contented. The man who said that "revolutions are not made with rose-water" was obviously inexperienced in practical human affairs. Men like Rousseau and Shelley do make revolutions, and do make them with rose-water; that is, with a too rosy and sentimental view of human goodness. Figures that come before and create convulsion and change (for instance, the central figure of the New Testament) always have the air of walking in an unnatural sweetness and calm. They give us their peace ultimately in blood and battle and division; not as the world giveth give they unto us.

Nor is the real reason of the triumph of the too-contented reformer particularly difficult to define. He triumphs because he keeps alive in the human soul an invincible sense of the thing being worth doing, of the war being worth winning, of the people being worth their deliverance. I remember that Mr. William Archer, some time ago, published in one of his interesting series of interviews, an interview with Mr. Thomas Hardy. That powerful writer was represented as saying, in the course of the conversation, that he did not wish at the particular moment to define his position with regard to the ultimate problem of whether life itself was worth living. There are, he said, hundreds of remediable evils in this world. When we have remedied all these (such was his argument), it will be time enough to ask whether existence itself under its best possible conditions is valuable or desirable. Here we have presented, with a considerable element of what can only be called unconscious humour, the plain reason of the failure of the pessimist as a reformer. Mr. Hardy is asking us, I will not say to buy a pig in a poke; he is asking us to buy a poke on the remote chance of there being a pig in it. When we have for some few frantic centuries tortured ourselves to save mankind, it will then be "time enough" to discuss whether they can possibly be saved. When, in the case of infant mortality, for example, we have exhausted ourselves with the earth-shaking efforts required to save the life of every individual baby, it will then be time enough to consider whether every individual baby would not have been happier dead. We are to remove mountains and bring the millennium, because then we can have a quiet

moment to discuss whether the millennium is at all
desirable.   Here we have the low-water mark of
the impotence of the sad reformer.   And here we
have the reason of the paradoxical triumph of the
happy one.   His triumph is a religious triumph;
it rests upon his perpetual assertion of the value
of the human soul and of human daily life.   It
rests upon his assertion that human life is enjoyable because it is human.   And he will never
admit, like so many compassionate pessimists, that
human life ever ceases to be human.   He does
not merely pity the lowness of men; he feels an
insult to their elevation.   Brute pity should be
given only to the brutes.   Cruelty to animals is
cruelty and a vile thing; but cruelty to a man is not
cruelty, it is treason.   Tyranny over a man is not
tyranny, it is rebellion, for man is royal.   Now,
the practical weakness of the vast mass of modern
pity for the poor and the oppressed is precisely
that it is merely pity; the pity is pitiful, but not
respectful.   Men feel that the cruelty to the poor
is a kind of cruelty to animals.   They never feel
that it is injustice to equals; nay, it is treachery
to comrades.   This dark, scientific pity, this brutal
pity, has an elemental sincerity of its own; but it
is entirely useless for all ends of social reform.
Democracy swept Europe with the sabre when

it was founded upon the Rights of Man. It has done literally nothing at all since it has been founded only upon the wrongs of man. Or, more strictly speaking, its recent failure has been due to its not admitting the existence of any rights or wrongs, or indeed of any humanity. Evolution (the sinister enemy of revolution) does not especially deny the existence of God ; what it does deny is the existence of man. And all the despair about the poor, and the cold and repugnant pity for them, has been largely due to the vague sense that they have literally relapsed into the state of the lower animals.

A writer sufficiently typical of recent revolutionism—Gorky—has called one of his books by the eerie and effective title " Creatures that once were Men." That title explains the whole failure of the Russian revolution. And the reason why the English writers, such as Dickens, did with all their limitations achieve so many of the actual things at which they aimed, was that they could not possibly have put such a title upon a human book. Dickens really helped the unfortunate in the matters to which he set himself. And the reason is that across all his books and sketches about the unfortunate might be written the common title, " Creatures that Still are Men."

There does exist, then, this strange optimistic reformer; the man whose work begins with approval and yet ends with earthquake. Jesus Christ was destined to found a faith which made the rich poorer and the poor richer; but even when He was going to enrich them, He began with the phrase, " Blessed are the poor." The Gissings and the Gorkys say, as an universal literary motto, "Cursed are the poor." Among a million who have faintly followed Christ in this divine contradiction, Dickens stands out especially. He said, in all his reforming utterances, "Cure poverty;" but he said in all his actual descriptions, " Blessed are the poor." He described their happiness, and men rushed to remove their sorrow. He described them as human, and men resented the insults to their humanity. It is not difficult to see why, as I said at an earlier stage of this book, Dickens's denunciations have had so much more practical an effect than the denunciations of such a man as Gissing. Both agreed that the souls of the people were in a kind of prison. But Gissing said that the prison was full of dead souls. Dickens said that the prison was full of living souls. And the fiery cavalcade of rescuers felt that they had not come too late.

Of this general fact about Dickens's descriptions

of poverty there will not, I suppose, be any serious dispute. The dispute will only be about the truth of those descriptions. It is clear that whereas Gissing would say, "See how their poverty depresses the Smiths or the Browns," Dickens says, "See how little, after all, their poverty can depress the Cratchits." No one will deny that he made a special feature a special study of the subject of the festivity of the poor. We will come to the discussion of the veracity of these scenes in a moment. It is here sufficient to register in conclusion of our examination of the reforming optimist, that Dickens certainly was such an optimist, and that he made it his business to insist upon what happiness there is in the lives of the unhappy. His poor man is always a Mark Tapley, a man the optimism of whose spirit increases if anything with the pessimism of his experience. It can also be registered as a fact equally solid and quite equally demonstrable that this optimistic Dickens did effect great reforms.

The reforms in which Dickens was instrumental were indeed, from the point of view of our sweeping social panaceas, special and limited. But perhaps, for that reason especially, they afford a compact and concrete instance of the psychological

paradox of which we speak.   Dickens did definitely
destroy—or at the very least help to destroy—certain institutions ; he destroyed those institutions
simply by describing them.   But the crux and
peculiarity of the whole matter is this, that, in a
sense, it can really be said that he described these
things too optimistically.   In a real sense, he described Dotheboys Hall as a better place than it is.
In a real sense, he made out the workhouse as a
pleasanter place than it can ever be.   For the
chief glory of Dickens is that he made these places
interesting ; and the chief infamy of England is
that it has made these places dull.   Dulness was
the one thing that Dickens's genius could never
succeed in describing ; his vitality was so violent
that he could not introduce into his books the
genuine impression even of a moment of monotony.
If there is anywhere in his novels an instant of
silence, we only hear more clearly the hero whis-
pering with the heroine, the villain sharpening his
dagger, or the creaking of the machinery that is to
give out the god from the machine.   He could
splendidly describe gloomy places, but he could
not describe dreary places.   He could describe
miserable marriages, but not monotonous marriages.   It must have been genuinely entertaining to
be married to Mr. Quilp.   This sense of a still

incessant excitement he spreads over every inch of
his story, and over every dark tract of his landscape. His idea of a desolate place is a place
where anything can happen ; he has no idea of that
desolate place where nothing can happen. This is
a good thing for his soul, for the place where nothing can happen is hell. But still, it might reason-
ably be maintained by the modern mind that he is
hampered in describing human evil and sorrow by
this inability to imagine tedium, this dulness in the
matter of dulness. For, after all, it is certainly
true that the worst part of the lot of the unfortunate is the fact that they have long spaces in which
to review the irrevocability of their doom. It is
certainly true that the worst days of the oppressed
man are the nine days out of ten in which he is not
oppressed. This sense of sickness and sameness
Dickens did certainly fail or refuse to give. When
we read such a description as that excellent one—
in detail—of Dotheboys Hall, we feel that, while
everything else is accurate, the author does, in the
words of the excellent Captain Nares in Stevenson's "Wrecker," "draw the dreariness rather
mild." The boys at Dotheboys were, perhaps, less
bullied, but they were certainly more bored. For,
indeed, how could any one be bored with the
society of so sumptuous a creature as Mr. Squeers?

Who would not put up with a few illogical floggings
in order to enjoy the conversation of a man
who could say, "She's a rum 'un is Natur'. . . .
Natur', is more easier conceived than described."
The same principle applies to the workhouse in
"Oliver Twist." We feel vaguely that neither
Oliver nor any one else could be entirely unhappy
in the presence of the purple personality of Mr.
Bumble. The one thing he did not describe in any
of the abuses he denounced was the soul-destroy-
ing potency of routine. He made out the bad
school, the bad parochial system, the bad debtor's
prison as very much jollier and more exciting than
they may really have been. In a sense, then, he
flattered them; but he destroyed them with the
flattery. By making Mrs. Gamp delightful he
made her impossible. He gave every one an interest in Mr. Bumble's existence; and by the same
act gave every one an interest in his destruction.
It would be difficult to find a stronger instance of
the utility and energy of the method which we
have, for the sake of argument, called the method
of the optimistic reformer. As long as low Yorkshire schools were entirely colourless and dreary,
they continued quietly tolerated by the public,
and quietly intolerable to the victims. So long
as Squeers was dull as well as cruel he was

permitted; the moment he became amusing as well
as cruel he was destroyed. As long as Bumble was
merely inhuman he was allowed. When he became human, humanity wiped him out. For in
order to do these great acts of justice we must
always realize not only the humanity of the oppressed, but even the humanity of the oppressor.
The satirist had, in a sense, to create the images in
the mind before, as an iconoclast, he could destroy
them. Dickens had to make Squeers live before he
could make him die.

In connection with the accusation of vulgar
optimism, which I have taken as a text for this
chapter, there is another somewhat odd thing to
notice. Nobody in the world was ever less optimistic than Dickens in his treatment of evil or the
evil man. When I say optimistic in this matter
I mean optimism, in the modern sense, of an
attempt to whitewash evil. Nobody ever made
less attempt to whitewash evil than Dickens. Nobody black was ever less white than Dickens's
black. He painted his villains and lost characters
more black than they really are. He crowds his
stories with a kind of villain rare in modern fiction
—the villain really without any "redeeming point."
There is no redeeming point in Squeers, or in
Monks, or in Ralph Nickleby, or in Bill Sikes, or

in Quilp, or in Brass, or in Mr. Chester, or in Mr. Pecksniff, or in Jonas Chuzzlewit, or in Carker, or in Uriah Heep, or in Blandois, or in a hundred more. So far as the balance of good and evil in human characters is concerned, Dickens certainly could not be called a vulgar optimist. His emphasis on evil was melodramatic. He might be called a vulgar pessimist.

Some will dismiss this lurid villainy as a detail of his artificial romance. I am not inclined to do so. He inherited, undoubtedly, this unqualified villain as he inherited so many other things, from the whole history of European literature. But he breathed into the blackguard a peculiar and vigorous life of his own. He did not show any tendency to modify his blackguardism in accordance with the increasing considerateness of the age; he did not seem to wish to make his villain less villainous; he did not wish to imitate the analysis of George Eliot, or the reverent scepticism of Thackeray. And all this works back, I think, to a real thing in him, that he wished to have an obstreperous and incalculable enemy. He wished to keep alive the idea of combat, which means, of necessity, a combat against something individual and alive. I do not know whether, in the kindly rationalism of his epoch, he kept any belief in a personal devil in his

theology, but he certainly created a personal devil
in every one of his books.

A good example of my meaning can be found,
for instance, in such a character as Quilp. Dickens
may, for all I know, have had originally some idea
of describing Quilp as the bitter and unhappy
cripple, a deformity whose mind is stunted along
with his body. But if he had such an idea, he soon
abandoned it. Quilp is not in the least unhappy.
His whole picturesqueness consists in the fact
that he has a kind of hellish happiness, an atrocious
hilarity that makes him go bounding about like an
indiarubber ball. Quilp is not in the least bitter;
he has an unaffected gaiety, an expansiveness, an
universality. He desires to hurt people in the
same hearty way that a good-natured man desires
to help them. He likes to poison people with the
same kind of clamorous camaraderie with which an
honest man likes to stand them drink. Quilp is not
in the least stunted in mind; he is not in reality
even stunted in body—his body, that is, does not in
any way fall short of what he wants it to do. His
smallness give him rather the promptitude of a
bird or the precipitance of a bullet. In a word,
Quilp is precisely the devil of the Middle Ages; he
belongs to that amazingly healthy period when
even the lost spirits were hilarious.

This heartiness and vivacity in the villains of Dickens is worthy of note because it is directly connected with his own cheerfulness. This is a truth little understood in our time, but it is a very essential one. If optimism means a general approval, it is certainly true that the more a man becomes an optimist the more he becomes a melancholy man. If he manages to praise everything, his praise will develop an alarming resemblance to a polite boredom. He will say that the marsh is as good as the garden; he will mean that the garden is as dull as the marsh. He may force himself to say that emptiness is good, but he will hardly prevent himself from asking what is the good of such good. This optimism does exist—this optimism which is more hopeless than pessimism—this optimism which is the very heart of hell. Against such an aching vacuum of joyless approval there is only one antidote—a sudden and pugnacious belief in positive evil. This world can be made beautiful again by beholding it as a battlefield. When we have defined and isolated the evil thing, the colours come back into everything else. When evil things have become evil, good things, in a blazing apocalypse, become good. There are some men who are dreary because they do not believe in God; but there are many others who are dreary because they do not believe in the devil. The grass grows green again when we believe in the devil, the roses grow red again when we believe in the devil.

No man was more filled with the sense of this bellicose basis of all cheerfulness than Dickens. He knew very well the essential truth, that the true optimist can only continue an optimist so long as he is discontented. For the full value of this life can only be got by fighting; the violent take it by storm. And if we have accepted everything, we have missed something—war. This life of ours is a very enjoyable fight, but a very miserable truce. And it appears strange to me that so few critics of Dickens or of other romantic writers have noticed this philosophical meaning in the undiluted villain. The villain is not in the story to be a character; he is there to be a danger—a ceaseless, ruthless, and uncompromising menace, like that of wild beasts or the sea. For the full satisfaction of the sense of combat, which everywhere and always involves a sense of equality, it is necessary to make the evil thing a man; but it is not always necessary, it is not even always artistic, to make him a mixed and probable man. In any tale, the tone of which is at all symbolic, he may quite legitimately be made an aboriginal and infernal energy. He must be a man only in the sense that he must have a wit and will to be matched with the wit and will of the man chiefly fighting. The evil may be inhuman, but it must not be impersonal, which is almost exactly the position occupied by Satan in the theological scheme.

But when all is said, as I have remarked before, the chief fountain in Dickens of what I have called cheerfulness, and some prefer to call optimism, is something deeper than a verbal philosophy. It is, after all, an incomparable hunger and pleasure for the vitality and the variety, for the infinite eccentricity of existence. And this word "eccentricity" brings us, perhaps, nearer to the matter than any other. It is, perhaps, the strongest mark of the divinity of man that he talks of this world as "a strange world," though he has seen no other. We feel that all there is is eccentric, though we do not know what is the centre. This sentiment of the grotesqueness of the universe ran through Dickens's brain and body like the mad blood of the elves. He saw all his streets in fantastic perspectives, he saw all his cockney villas as top heavy and wild, he saw every man's nose twice as big as it was, and every man's eyes like saucers. And this was the basis of his gaiety—the only real basis of any philosophical gaiety. This world is not to be justified as it is justified by the mechanical

optimists; it is not to be justified as the best of all
possible worlds.   Its merit is not that it is orderly
and explicable; its merit is that it is wild and
utterly unexplained.   Its merit is precisely that
none of us could have conceived such a thing, that
we should have rejected the bare idea of it as
miracle and unreason.   It is the best of all impossible worlds.

CHAPTER XII

A NOTE ON THE FUTURE OF DICKENS

THE hardest thing to remember about our own time, of course, is simply that it is a time; we all instinctively think of it as the Day of Judgment. But all the things in it which belong to it merely as this time will probably be rapidly turned upside down; all the things that can pass will pass. It is not merely true that all old things are already dead; it is also true that all new things are already dead; for the only undying things are the things that are neither new nor old. The more you are up with this year's fashion, the more (in a sense) you are already behind next year's. Consequently, in attempting to decide whether an author will, as it is cantly expressed, live, it is necessary to have very firm convictions about what part, if any part, of man is unchangeable. And it is very hard to have this if you have not a religion or, at least, a dogmatic philosophy.

The equality of men needs preaching quite as much as regards the ages as regards the classes of men. To feel infinitely superior to a man in

the twelfth century is just precisely as snobbish
as to feel infinitely superior to a man in the Old
Kent Road. There are differences between the
man and us, there may be superiorities in us over
the man; but our sin in both cases consists in
thinking of the small things wherein we differ
when we ought to be confounded and intoxicated
by the terrible and joyful matters in which we
are at one. But here again the difficulty always
is that the things near us seem larger than they
are, and so seem to be a permanent part of
mankind, when they may really be only one of
its parting modes of expression. Few people,
for instance, realize that a time may easily come
when we shall see the great outburst of Science
in the nineteenth century as something quite as
splendid, brief, unique, and ultimately abandoned,
as the outburst of Art at the Renascence. Few
people realize that the general habit of fiction, of
telling tales in prose, may fade, like the general
habit of the ballad, of telling tales in verse, has for
the time faded. Few people realize that reading
and writing are only arbitrary, and perhaps temporary sciences, like heraldry.

The immortal mind will remain, and by that
writers like Dickens will be securely judged. That
Dickens will have a high place in permanent

literature there is, I imagine, no prig surviving to
deny.   But though all prediction is in the dark,
I would devote this chapter to suggesting that his
place in nineteenth-century England will not only
be high, but altogether the highest.   At a certain
period of his contemporary fame, an average
Englishman would have said that there were at
that moment in England about five or six able and
equal novelists.   He could have made a list,
Dickens, Bulwer Lytton, Thackeray, Charlotte
Brontë, George Eliot, perhaps more.   Forty years
or more have passed and some of them have
slipped to a lower place.   Some would now say
tl t the highest platform is left to Thackeray and
Dickens; some to Dickens, Thackery, and George
Eliot; some to Dickens, Thackeray, and Charlotte
Brontë.   I venture to offer the proposition that
when more years have passed and more weeding has been effected, Dickens will dominate the
whole England of the nineteenth century; he will
be left on that platform alone.

I know that this is an almost impertinent thing
to assert, and that its tendency is to bring in
those disparaging discussions of other writers in
which Mr. Swinburne brilliantly embroiled himself
in his suggestive study of Dickens.   But my dis-
paragement of the other English Novelists is wholly

relative and not in the least positive. It is certain
that men will always return to such a writer as
Thackeray, with his rich emotional autumn, his
feeling that life is a sad but sacred retrospect, in
which at least we should forget nothing. It is not
likely that wise men will forget him. So, for
instance, wise and scholarly men do from time to
time return to the lyrists of the French Renascence,
to the delicate poignancy of Du Bellay : so they will
go back to Thackeray. But I mean that Dickens
will bestride and dominate our time as the vast
figure of Rabelais dominates Du Bellay, dominates
the Renascence and the world.

Yet we put a negative reason first. The particular things for which Dickens is condemned
(and justly condemned) by his critics, are precisely
those things which have never prevented a man
from being immortal. The chief of them is the
unquestionable fact that he wrote an enormous
amount of bad work. This does lead to a man
being put below his place in his own time : it does
not affect his permanent place, to all appearance,
at all. Shakespeare, for instance, and Wordsworth
wrote not only an enormous amount of bad work,
but an enormous amount of enormously bad work.
Humanity edits such writers' works for them.
Virgil was mistaken in cutting out his inferior

lines; we would have undertaken the job. Moreover in the particular case of Dickens there are
special reasons for regarding his bad work, as in
some sense, irrelevant. So much of it was written,
as I have previously suggested, under a kind of
general ambition that had nothing to do with his
special genius; an ambition to be a public provider
of everything, a warehouse of all human emotions.
He held a kind of literary day of judgment. He
distributed bad characters as punishments and
good characters as rewards. My meaning can be
best conveyed by one instance out of many. The
character of the kind old Jew in "Our Mutual
Friend" (a needless and unconvincing character)
was actually introduced because some Jewish
correspondent complains that the bad old Jew in
"Oliver Twist" conveyed the suggestion that all
Jews were bad. The principle is so light-headedly
absurd that it is hard to imagine any literary man
submitting to it for an instant. If ever he invented
a bad auctioneer he must immediately balance him
with a good auctioneer; if he should have conceived an unkind philanthropist, he must on the
spot, with whatever natural agony and toil,
imagine a kind philanthropist. The complaint is
frantic; yet Dickens, who tore people in pieces
for much fairer complaints, liked this complaint

of his Jewish correspondent. It pleased him to
be mistaken for a public arbiter : it pleased him to
be asked (in a double sense) to judge Israel. All
this is so much another thing, a non-literary
vanity, that there is much less difficulty than usual
in separating it from his serious genius : and by
his serious genius, I need hardly say, I mean his
comic genius. Such irrelevant ambitions as this
are easily passed over, like the sonnets of great
statesmen. We feel that such things can be set
aside, as the ignorant experiments of men otherwise great, like the politics of Professor Tyndall or
the philosophy of Professor Haeckel. Hence, I
think, posterity will not care that Dickens has done
bad work, but will know that he has done good.

Again, the other chief accusation against Dickens
was that his characters and their actions were
exaggerated and impossible. But this only meant
that they were exaggerated and impossible as compared with the modern world and with certain
writers (like Thackeray or Trollope) who were
making a very exact copy of the manners of the
modern world. Some people, oddly enough, have
suggested that Dickens has suffered or will suffer
from the change of manners. Surely this is
irrational. It is not the creators of the impossible
who will suffer from the process of time : Mr.

Bunsby can never be any more impossible than he was when Dickens made him. The writers who will obviously suffer from time will be the careful and realistic writers; the writers who have observed every detail of the fashion of this world which passeth away. It is surely obvious that there is nothing so fragile as a fact, that a fact flies away quicker than a fancy. A fancy will endure for two thousand years. For instance, we all have fancy for an entirely fearless man, a hero: and the Achilles of Homer still remains. But exactly the thing we do not know about Achilles is how far he was possible. The realistic narrators of the time are all forgotten (thank God) so we cannot tell whether Homer slightly exaggerated or wildly exaggerated or did not exaggerate at all, the personal activity of a Mycenæan captain in battle: for the fancy has survived the facts. So the fancy of Podsnap may survive the facts of English commerce: and no one will know whether Podsnap was possible, but only know that he is desirable, like Achilles.

The positive argument for the permanence of Dickens comes back to the thing that can only be stated and cannot be discussed: creation. He made things which nobody else could possibly make. He made Dick Swiveller in a very

different sense to that in which Thackeray made
Colonel Newcome. Thackeray's creation was
observation: Dickens's was poetry, and is therefore permanent. But there is one other test that
can be added. The immortal writer, I conceive, is
commonly he who does something universal in a
special manner. I mean that he does something
interesting to all men in a way in which only one
man or one land can do. Other men in that land,
who do only what other men in other lands are
doing as well, tend to have a great reputation
in their day and to sink slowly into a second or
a third or a fourth place. A parallel from war will
make the point clearer. I cannot think that any one
will doubt that, although Wellington and Nelson
were always bracketed, Nelson will steadily become
more important and Wellington less. For the
fame of Wellington rests upon the fact that he was
a good soldier in the service of England, exactly
as twenty similar men were good soldiers in the
service of Austria or Prussia or France. But
Nelson is the symbol of a special mode of attack,
which is at once universal and yet specially English,
the sea. Now Dickens is at once as universal as
the sea and as English as Nelson. Thackeray and
George Eliot and the other great figures of that
great England, were comparable to Wellington in

this, that the kind of thing they were doing,—
realism, the acute study of intellectual things,
numerous men in France, Germany and Italy were
doing as well or better than they. But Dickens
was really doing something universal, yet something that no one but an Englishmen could do.
This is attested by the fact that he and Byron are
the men who, like pinnacles, strike the eye of the
continent. The points would take long to study :
yet they may take only a moment to indicate. No
one but an Englishman could have filled his books
at once with a furious caricature and with a
positively furious kindness. In more central
countries, full of cruel memories of political change,
caricature is always inhumane. No one but an
Englishman could have described the democracy
as consisting of free men, but yet of funny men.
In other countries where the democratic issue has
been more bitterly fought, it is felt that unless
you describe a man as dignified you are describing
him as a slave. This is the only final greatness of
a man; that he does for all the world what all
the world cannot do for itself. Dickens, I believe,
did it.

The hour of absinthe is over. We shall not be
much further troubled with the little artists who
found Dickens too sane for their sorrows and too

clean for their delights. But we have a long way to travel before we get back to what Dickens meant: and the passage is along a rambling English road, a twisting road such as Mr. Pickwick travelled. But this at least is part of what he meant; that comradeship and serious joy are not interludes in our travel; but that rather our travels are interludes in comradeship and joy, which through God shall endure for ever. The inn does not point to the road; the road points to the inn. And all roads point at last to an ultimate inn, where we shall meet Dickens and all his characters: and when we drink again it shall be from the great flagons in the tavern at the end of the world.

INDEX

A

Agnes, 267, 268
Allen, Miss, 97
" American Notes," 136, 146
Anglo-Saxonism, 151, 152
Archer, William, 272
Austen, Jane, 126, 238

B

Bagstock, Major, 19, 81, 185, 185 *seq.*
" Barnaby Rudge," 124, 125
Barnacles, 62, 63, 224
Beardsley, Aubrey, 18
Betsy, 226
Blackmore, Mr., 57
" Bleak House," 200 *seq.*, 227, 236
Boffin, 81, 87
Bounderby, 224, 228
Brass, Sally, 168, 282
Braybrooke, Lord, 114
British Constitution, 61, 222
Brontë, Charlotte, 4, 290
Browne, H. K. (Phiz), 74, 110
Browning, Robert, 68
Bucket, 204
Bumble, 101, 133, 148, 280, 281
Bunsby, Mr., 17, 110, 194
Burns, Robert, 41, 245
Buzfuz, 211
Byron, Lord, 42, 296

C

Carker, Mr., 183, 282
Carlyle, Thomas, 2, 4, 11, 224, 230, 231, 232
Carlyle, Mrs., 59, 210
Catholic Church, 153, 155, 236
Century, early nineteenth, 7 *seq.*, 132
Chadband, 130, 168, 221, 224
Chamberlain, 126
Chapman and Hall, 73, 78, 79, 118
Chaucer, 160
Chesterton, Captain, 146, 147
" Child's History of England," 159
" Chimes, The," 157, 171 *seq.*
Chollop, 110, 147
Christianity, 13, 100
" Christmas Carol," 21, 166, 168, 169 *seq.*
Chuckster, 57, 181, 188, 261
Church of England, 217
Circumlocution Office, 61 *seq.*, 81
Clennam, 168, 230
Cobbett, 6
Collins, Wilkie, 227
Copyright laws, 138, 143
Corelli, Marie, 100
Court of Chancery, 200, 269
" Cricket on the Hearth," 176 *seq.*
Crisparkle, 180, 218
Cromwell, Oliver, 10, 11